WHITE TO WHITE ON BLACK/WHITE

To Linda,
    Thanks for caring.
I know you'll make
a difference.
    Yours in the Struggle,
    Toni E. Weaver

Proceeds from this printing will be used for further educational materials to help in the understanding and elimination of racism in America.

"The problem, then, for those who would prefer a more just society is to recognize that they have not been exempted from America's racism and to deal with it openly."

Alphonso Pinkney
The Myth of Black Progress

WHITE TO WHITE

ON

BLACK/WHITE

This is an educational and motivational handbook for whites who want to know how racism is perpetuated in America and how they contribute to the problem. Whites' most often asked questions on Black/white relations are addressed and potential ways to become a part of the solution are offered.

Toni E. Weaver, Ph.D.

First Edition

Voices Publishing, Vandalia, Ohio

WHITE TO WHITE ON BLACK/WHITE

By Toni E. Weaver, Ph.D.

Published by:
Voices Publishing
Post Office Box 13
Vandalia, OH 45377-0013, U.S.A.

Library of Congress Catalog Card Number 93-60293
    Weaver, Toni E.
    White to White on Black/White

ISBN 0-9636543-7-3   Soft Cover

ACKNOWLEDGMENT

In addition to those researchers and authors on race relations who came before me, I would like to acknowledge Anna Weems' and Claudia Pattison's persistent support and promotion of our seminars.

I am also indebted to those people who previewed the first draft of this manuscript and shared their honest feelings and criticisms with me. Thanks to: Dr. Edward Wingard, Dr. Doug Davidson, Dr. Minnie Johnson, Dr. Wally Sikes, Dr. Twyla Respress, Dr. George Schulz, Sherry Schneider, James Orrill, Curtis Wingard, Brian Wingard, Mark Perry, Miriam Riggins, Claudia Chambers, Bryan Wheeler and Dr. Barbara Beck.

My sincere thanks also to Claudia Chambers for her flawless typesetting and supportive attitude and to Gloria Wingard's conscientious editing.

I'm appreciative of James P. Orrill and C & O Printing Company's technical assistance on printing and Michael E. Weaver's cover graphics.

Cover by Michael E. Weaver

WARNING - DISCLAIMER

This book is designed to provide information in regard to the subject matter covered.

Every effort has been made to make this manual as accurate as possible. However, there may be mistakes both typographical and in content.

The purpose of this manual is to educate and motivate. The author and Voices Publishing shall have neither liability nor responsibility to any person or entity with respect to any loss or damage caused or alleged to be caused directly or indirectly by the information contained in this book.

WARNING - DISCLAIMER

DEDICATION

Thousands of people are responsible for this book; I especially dedicate it to:

- My late husband, Larry E. Weaver, Sr. and my four caring children, Elaina, Matthew, Michael and Larry, Jr. whose support and understanding allowed me to share my new learnings with so many others and whose attitudes and actions continue to keep me hopeful for the future.

- The late Dr. Charles H. King, Jr., a beautiful African-American man who made me aware that I was part of the problem of racism in America, inspired me to become part of the solution and mentored me as we developed the second day of the workshop he created on racism.

- Dr. C.T. Vivian, whose sacrifices and commitment to the struggle for civil rights as an African-American man has impacted so many; working with him has greatly enhanced my knowledge, my soul, and made it possible for me to have an influence on so many.

- The thousands of participants in the Urban Crisis and Urban Potential Seminars:

    - The African-Americans who shared with us so lovingly their pain and struggle to survive in a racist culture and who sent me pictures of their babies to keep me inspired.

    - The white Americans who were open and caring enough to rethink their value systems and who promised to become a part of the solution.

    - The many other people who also have felt the pain of discrimination and began to see that our unity is a big part of the solution.

-       The out-front racists who could not open their minds or hearts; their contribution of negative attitudes exposed racism and moved many whites to become a part of the solution.

TABLE OF CONTENTS

- Why are Blacks so angry? It makes whites more fearful.
- Why do Blacks always sit together?
- I try to be friendly, why do Blacks act like they have a "chip" on their shoulder?
- Why do Blacks not trust me just because I'm white?
- In school, Blacks treated me badly; why do they pick on whites?

- I have Black friends; how can I be part of the problem?
- What's the big deal? I work with Blacks and we get along.
- I have Black friends; why haven't they told me of their daily problems with whites?
- We all fear people who are different, don't we?
- What does color matter? I don't look at color, only the person.
- If we all loved one another, we wouldn't have this problem, would we?

- Why do Blacks kill each other?
- Why are there more crime and drugs in the Black community?

PREFACE

Since 1970, I have worked in Black/white relations. I helped to write and pass an Ordinance against discrimination in my city, helped form a Speaker's Bureau on discrimination and served as chair of their first Human Relations Commission. Since 1972, I have been co-teaching, as the white part of a Black/white team, a two-day seminar that really helps white people to understand the pervasiveness of racism in their own lives and makes them want to change their own attitudes and challenge others to do the same.

Through these seminars, which I helped to develop, I have come in contact with thousands of people (white and Black) who have shared their personal, racial experiences with me. Over the past twenty years, I have learned how whites and Blacks view and interact with each other and discovered how little white people really know about how the system of racism operates.

This book is my way of sharing some of the things that I have learned with other whites who won't be as fortunate as I have been to see a new vision for America when we rid ourselves of racism and sexism.

From my research of literature in the area of race relations in America, I have noticed that most books written on racism or Black/white relations tend to focus on history or theories and analyses of the problem, but seldom offer ways to deal with the people or institutions that perpetuate it. There are few books written for the general public; most are textbooks or geared for professional social scientists.

Therefore, this book will not focus on history, theories or analyses, but will be written in terms that the average American can understand.

It also will not go in depth on statistics. The bibliography includes other references for history, theories and statistics; more detailed reading can also be found there. I have compiled a list of the questions white people ask most often in our seminars on the Black/white issue and this book will focus on information that will help whites answer those questions for themselves and/or others.

The main thing that most of us can do is to affect the

13

people we come in contact with, which will eventually change society. My intent is to impart information that will help you deal with the people you hear making prejudicial comments and to give some suggestions about other things that can be done in your family, community, schools, businesses, churches and organizations to stop the perpetuation of racism in any areas in which you have some influence.

If we all began to do those small things we can do, we could begin to eliminate the racism in America; after all, individuals do make up our institutions and do change them when necessary.

I will be focusing on Black/white issues because these have been continuously difficult for most white Americans to overcome. However, the basic principles apply to all who are discriminated against in America, whether they are people of color, females, Jewish, elderly, physically challenged, gay or lesbian.

It is my hope that you will also learn enough to "stand up" to any form of discrimination when it appears.

I also will be using both the terms Black and African-American interchangeably as we are still in a transition period between the two terms. I capitalize Black and not white because Black is a term that African-Americans choose in their search for identity in America. White is a collective term assigned to people who are not Black.

Some basic things to keep in mind as you read this book that will help you understand my perspective on racism are listed below:

1. My view may seem one-sided because racism in America is basically only perpetuated by one side!

2. For the most part, all that Blacks in America can do is to <u>react</u> to the racist system since racism keeps them from being in control enough to <u>act</u>. Everything important that Blacks do has to take into account that they are operating in a racist system.

3. All African-Americans do not think alike! However, under an oppressive system like ours, most have

many of the same experiences with whites which causes them to have many of the same reactions to racism.

4. The purpose of this book is not to make whites feel guilty but to motivate them to understand and act. I also understand that Blacks are responsible for their behavior in spite of the racism. We must both change and be able to communicate our feelings honestly to each other. However, since whites are in the majority and in control, they also have the most responsibility for initiating change.

5. In America, there are exceptions to most everything. I am necessarily speaking to what happens in general; nothing is 100%.

6. This book is only a small piece of the solution; it is intended to be motivational and informative to a general white audience who do not see themselves as racist nor understand the magnitude of the problem. I hope other authors will deal with other aspects of the issue.

"To get the bad customs of a country changed and new ones, tho better, introduced, it is necessary first to remove the prejudice of the people, enlighten their ignorance and convince them that their interests will be promoted by the proposed changes; and this is not the work of a day."

Benjamin Franklin, 1781

INTRODUCTION

I ended up a white racist by default! Though I never did anything on purpose to hurt any person of color, my ignorance and passivity allowed me to get advantages from a system that did it for me.

I was fortunate to find out how I was a part of the problem which caused me to want to be part of the solution.

I began to realize that the real problem with racism in America is not the outright bigot but is, in fact, largely good white people who don't see themselves as racist but who end up as part of a system that destroys people of color, especially African-Americans.

It is my belief that most whites do not want to be racist or participate in a system that does it for them. Pettigrew estimates that only 15% of whites are anti-Black, 25% are for Blacks and 60% of whites simply conform to the system that does it for them.[1] I want to share with you some of what I've learned so that you too can do your part in the elimination of racism in America.

When I refer to the system or institutional racism, I'm speaking of the patterns of behavior that whites exhibit as a result of our first, most basic institution, the family. We are taught that we are white Americans with the implication that white is superior. We carry these racist assumptions and resulting behaviors and thought patterns to all of our other institutions. For example, there are banks that red-line areas where they won't make loans, school counselors who lead African-American children into classes that do not prepare them for going to college, churches that portray Jesus and the disciples as white, and realtors who steer African-Americans away from white areas. Consequently, African-Americans must be strong enough to compete on white terms and to overcome the negativity that whites place on dark skin color.

Remember that racism continues in America because the system conditions us to dislike each other. No one of color in America is treated as fairly as white people, and yet other people of color are encouraged to be prejudiced against the group less acceptable than they are.

Many of our ancestors came to America as immigrants

17

and were treated very badly. (There were signs that said "Irish and dogs keep off the grass" and some Italians created the Mafia as a way to survive in a culture that treated them as less than human.) Yet many of those immigrants who were hated became prejudiced against people of color in order to be accepted themselves.

If we put together all those groups who are and have been discriminated against, we would have a majority and could rid ourselves of the racism which causes America to be less productive than it could be. We can turn the peer pressure around and make it unpopular to be a racist. When people are challenged on any remark that puts others down, they have to think twice before saying it again. If all whites who don't consider themselves to be racist just stood up to those who are, we would see a drastic improvement in Black/white relations.

I think that before we can deal with other white people on their prejudice, we must first be honest with ourselves.

The truth is that if you grew up in America and are white, you are a rare exception if you're not prejudiced against people of color, especially Blacks. Oh sure, you may be less prejudiced than others but deep down when you're honest with yourself, you know you have some negative attitudes or stereotypical thoughts when a person of color, especially a Black, approaches; and even though you may be all for the rights of Blacks, you don't want your children to marry "one".

For those of you who are still saying "I'm really not prejudiced", chances are you don't challenge those who are! You may walk away from racists but few whites let others know why their jokes weren't funny or that we were offended by their remarks.

Most whites have the capacity to empathize with being mistreated since most have had some instances of not being treated fairly. This book will help you begin to see what it means to have your color seen as a negative trait on a daily basis.

Chapter I

Treatment - Black to White

- **Why are Blacks so angry? It makes whites more fearful.**

Anger is a human response to continued mistreatment. If someone came up to you daily and hit you because they didn't like the way you looked, would you not be angry?

African-Americans continue to be oppressed daily because of individual and institutionalized racism. Many African-Americans in the 1990's are still experiencing individual daily slights such as clerks putting the change on the counter so they don't have to touch the person; being followed in stores as though all Blacks are shoplifters (the real shoplifters often work in Black-White teams knowing that the Black will be followed while the white person does the shoplifting); being pulled over by the police for no apparent reason and being spread-eagled on the car; seeing whites clutch their purses and/or their children when they walk by; watching whites cross the street when they see you (especially if you're a young Black male); having salespeople wait on the white person while ignoring you. While it may be true that sometimes Blacks see these slights as being racially-motivated when they are not, they happen often enough that Blacks always have to question whether or not they were done because of racism. Many African-Americans have shared with me their ways of making clear, when they can, whether or not they're being treated differently. Sometimes, Blacks will move around in a store in such a way that makes it obvious that they are being followed or they will go out of their way to make sure the clerk sees them if they are being ignored.

I know a white man who questioned a security guard in a large department store about why he wasn't stopped when he came in with a shopping bag while the Black man who came in right after him with a bag was stopped. The guard said it was the Blacks who shoplifted!

On an institutional basis, most African-Americans experience injustice at work in many different ways. They watch whites with less education or experience being promoted over them (often whites they trained); when they present an idea in a meeting, it is not acknowledged but when a white person makes the same suggestion later, it is accepted as a good idea (much the same thing happens to white women as well); when a job becomes available in the department, Blacks are often asked to fill in but during the search process are never considered for the position; they are written up for infractions that whites are not written up for, and whatever education Blacks have, whites act as though it wasn't as good as theirs or that it wasn't achieved on merit.

The anger of Blacks lessened after the Civil Rights Era produced new laws to end discrimination; the change in laws also raised expectations that treatment would now be fair and steady progress would eventually equalize opportunities. Since these laws were never really enforced, the progress that was made was only temporary. The figures in most major areas have gone backwards (especially since 1980) to where they were before the laws were changed. This regression only served to dash the hopes African-Americans had for future equal treatment and increased their anger.

I'm seeing more open, serious expressions of anger in the 1990's from young African-Americans who did everything that society says you are supposed to do to make it in America. They worked hard, got an education in spite of the racism and were well-dressed and well-mannered. After a few years in the workplace, they are very depressed and angry to find that they are not seen or treated the same as their young, white counterparts.

African-Americans grow up learning how to control their anger and do a very good job of it for the most part. When whites see Blacks letting their anger out, it often seems as though they are over-reacting to a small incident because they don't know the daily accumulation of experiences that have been recurring over a long period of time that they have held inside. Eventually when Blacks blow up at a seemingly small incident, they are seen as over-sensitive.

Perhaps whites are fearful because on some level they know the anger is justified! To say the Black-white problem is caused by African-Americans being angry is to blame the victim. The only way to diffuse this anger is to be honest about the cause of it (white racism), and for whites to be angry that our system is not living up to its laws or its stated values of "liberty and justice for all". It is not realistic to ask people not to be angry when they are regularly treated as less than human!

- Why do Blacks always sit together?

Interestingly enough, this is one area that whites most often cite as to how they see the problem manifested at work and school.

I've always found it fascinating that whites seldom mention that whites usually all sit together. If whites really wanted to solve this problem, all they would have to do is to sit down with some Blacks.

Have you noticed women also tend to group together at lunch and parties? We tend to take women being together for granted; however, we tend to forget that in the past it was not acceptable for women to join men in many social occasions and if they did, had to suffer many putdowns and indignities.

Much the same is true with African-Americans. Most have been so rejected when they tried to join white people or

21

had to put up with so many put-downs that many eventually gave up trying. When you have to put up with being treated as less than human on the job, you at least want to spend your lunch hour or social time with people who treat you as a full human being. If you're listening to remarks all day that put you down, you naturally stay away from those people in your free time, and try to create networks that are supportive of you.

Remember that Blacks have their own churches, sororities and fraternities and Miss Black America contests only because the white groups either did not allow them in or did not allow them full participation.

Black churches began because white churches made African-Americans sit in a separate area and did not allow them to take communion or pray with whites at the altar. When Blacks started their own churches, they welcomed whites who were willing to worship together. I've been to Black churches and the welcome I've had was in total contrast to what I've seen when a Black comes to a white church. I even know a white man who went to a Black church he found in the woods while he was on a hunting trip and in hunting clothes. He said he was made to feel totally welcome! I find it hard to imagine the opposite if it was a Black hunter in a white church.

Remember, there are always exceptions to anything. In general, white people in a Black church are treated better than they deserve; they are welcomed, acknowledged, and often asked to return with their family and friends. In most white churches, when a Black family shows up, they are treated civilly but the questions are usually geared towards finding out if they're just visiting or do they plan to come back; do they have children and how old are the children? As long as Blacks are just visiting, they are tolerated. If there is the possibility that the family may return and join the church, the reception is most often not so friendly. If a Black family joins the church, then they must be accepted as full human beings. We also know some white churches who have actually turned Blacks away who came to worship.

Fraternities and sororities have always been very

exclusive; even white students without the proper background or sponsorship were not accepted. In more recent times, a Black may have been accepted but that was the exception. So African-Americans naturally formed their own sororities or fraternities as a way of having a social life and a support system in a white environment that did not accept them. Even when Blacks form their own organizations, they almost all have some white participation and do not refuse white membership.

Though we've never called the Miss America contest a white contest, it has always been that. We usually had a minority woman among the finalists but not as a winner until the late 80's and even the African-American women who won, with rare exception, were largely representative of white beauty, not Black beauty.

I've always been amazed that in The Miss Universe contest they have many beautiful women of color and yet the finalists are all white except for one or two. Three-quarters of the world are people of color! If it were a fair contest, one would expect a Miss Universe contest to have, as finalists, largely women of color and maybe one or two white women.

We have forced people of color to create their own networks and contests as the only way most can have a real chance to compete on their own merits. Blacks basically have not been separatists and those who have tried to be have not had a large following, though they do get a lot of publicity.

The truth is even if Blacks want to give up on white people, in a majority white system, they cannot survive without participating in the mainstream of our society.

- **I try to be friendly, why do Blacks act like they have a chip on their shoulder?**

- **Why do Blacks not trust me just because I'm white?**

White to White on Black/White

Sometimes when whites try to treat Blacks as just another person, they are rebuffed. It only takes a time or two for most whites to get discouraged and say Blacks have a `chip' on their shoulder and don't trust whites. Many whites are hurt that Blacks would mistrust them without knowing them first.

What we need to understand is that most whites end up prejudiced in America,[2] often without even realizing it and most Blacks have daily experiences that reinforce their feelings that whites are not to be trusted.

Many Blacks have shared personal experiences with me on their relationships with whites. One of the things that quite often happens is a Black woman and a white woman will become friends at work and the Black woman begins to trust the white woman; they may even go to lunch together. Then one week-end the Black woman is at the mall and sees the white woman with her husband (or a white friend). The Black woman comes over to say "hi" and the white woman turns away from her as though she doesn't know her. Back at work the white woman continues to be friendly and either pretends like nothing happened or in some cases actually tells the Black woman not to speak to her outside of work when she is with her friends! Who needs friends like that? The Black woman may be very cold to the next white woman who tries to be friendly to avoid being hurt again. Of course, many Blacks do have white friends who prove over a period of time that they are real all the time, not just in certain circumstances.

Many women have a similar reaction to males. They are very cautious with men until they have a reason to trust; when you've been hurt, you don't trust again easily.

- **In school, Blacks treated me badly; why do they pick on whites?**

Often, the first time that whites came into daily contact with African-Americans was in an integrated high school.

24

Treatment - Black to White

There was usually a lot of pressure on both sides to stay only with your group.

Blacks have seen that white students are treated better by most white teachers while Blacks are assumed to be not as bright and more violent. I've had a number of white teachers admit that when they see Black students playing around in the hall that they have a disgusted attitude about it while white students doing the same thing are seen as just having fun.

School dances have often been a source of anger and frustration for African-American students as well. The proms often have themes that are insulting to the Black students (like glorifying the southern plantation system of slavery, displaying the Confederate flag or focusing on square dancing).

Even in athletics where Blacks are prominent, often the cheerleaders are mostly white. It has been looked down on for Blacks and whites to date or socialize together. Some Black athletes were even told by their coaches not to date white women.

So even though many high schools are technically integrated, there has been little or no effort to bring the students together or in many cases for Blacks to have the same representation on committees which decide the social environment. The Blacks band together as a way of protecting themselves which is frightening to the white students who usually do not understand what the Blacks have been through.

So when a white has a bad experience with a Black, there is a tendency to blame all Blacks for it. If a white student did the same thing to a white, the blame would only be on that student, not all whites. When you live in a racist society, anything that is negative tends to reinforce the stereotypes.

CONCLUSION

Since racism is institutionalized in America, most whites end up prejudiced without even thinking about it. The regular assault of white individuals and institutions upon African-Americans causes them to be defensive, mistrusting and angry.

Even though we technically have integrated schools, the students are very much segregated and little attempt has been made to form positive interaction between Blacks and whites.

The Black or white students who try to bridge this gap are often ostracized by their peer groups since most students feel that their survival depends on sticking together.

Chapter 2

Treatment - White to Black

- I have Black friends; how can I be part
  of the problem?

- What's the big deal? I work with Blacks
  and we get along.

- I have Black friends. Why haven't they
  told me their daily problems with
  whites?

Though many whites say they work with Blacks and
have Black friends, they usually do not know what African–
Americans go through on a daily basis; they often use these
relationships as a credit card, as a way of saying that they're
not part of the problem.

Usually the Blacks they consider as friends and co-
workers do not share their daily personal experiences and
mistreatment with them.   When African-Americans have
attempted to tell whites what they're experiencing, too often it
makes the white uncomfortable and hurts the relationship;
whites often tell Blacks that they're over-sensitive or say the
same thing happens to whites too! Eventually most Blacks give
up on trying to explain their situations.

Do you think about your color everyday from the time
you get up in the morning? If you're white, you usually don't;

only a serious bigot or a white working in a mostly Black environment even gives it a thought. If you're an African-American, you have to be conscious on a daily basis of your color because people treat you differently because of it. One Black male I know explained it by saying that one day he got up and left the house without even thinking about his color; he said he wasn't out of the house for half an hour before a white person did something to remind him of it! So, it's not a choice for most African-Americans; it's also not their color that is the problem! The problem is that white people treat them differently because of their color. Blacks have to be prepared to respond; their survival in a racist culture depends upon it.

I would suggest that if you have Black friends who have not shared their experiences and pain from racist treatment with you that they are more acquaintances than friends. It is up to whites to be more aware of what is happening and bring up the subject with the Blacks they are close to; it's been my experience that African-Americans are more than willing to share when they see you are really trying to understand.

Too often whites use their Black friends as credit cards to show how liberal they are or treat Blacks in a patronizing way as though they were children who need to be taken care of - we want to feed people to make ourselves feel better but seldom do we go the next step and actually do something that makes it possible for people to feed themselves. African-Americans don't want us to give them a hand-out; they only want an equal chance to succeed or fail on their own merits.

For the future, it will not be a matter of what we do for Blacks that will make the difference, it will be what we do with whites that matters. White Americans control the system that perpetuates racism and if we don't change the system, then we cannot change the condition that surrounds African-Americans.

It's also been my experience that the only way that Blacks really believe whites are serious is when they see us stand up to other whites about their racism. You can't just say you're o.k., you have to prove it by your actions, and uncompromising convictions.

Treatment - White to Black

In the workplace, it often looks like everyone is getting along when in fact most whites have learned to tolerate working with Blacks, but have not necessarily accepted Blacks fully or socially outside of the workplace.

- **We all fear people who are different or unknown, don't we?**

White people often act as though it is natural to fear people who are different than they are or to fear what they don't understand.

If that were true, most of us would be afraid of Frenchmen. However, when we have a Frenchman at our parties, we're fascinated by his differences. We ask him to say things in French that we don't understand because we love the way he sounds; we ask lots of questions about how French people live and act.

If someone came to you and said she had a panic attack every time she saw a red-headed person because she thought she would be robbed or raped, you would tell her to seek psychological counseling!

Yet, many white people think it is perfectly normal to fear people who have color in their skin. To me, that attitude also reflects a psychological impairment. There are things we should be afraid of in America but being fearful just because a person has color in their skin is not one of them. I have found it to be a very freeing experience to rid myself of this unreasonable fear.

It's not so much that we fear difference as it is that we fear what we have been taught is a negative difference. The culture, especially the media, continues to condition us with negative attitudes towards people of color and towards Black males in particular.

Practically every night on the news we see Black males in handcuffs; eventually this sets up an unconscious fear that Black males are criminals. When they talk about welfare, they most often show Blacks as the recipients even though, in numbers and dollars, the vast majority are white.

The Blacks we know who don't fit these stereotypes are seen as exceptions, not the rule, while white people who are criminals or welfare recipients are seen as the exception, not the rule.

If we began to educate our children on what racism is and how it continues to keep African-Americans from fully participating in our society, they would understand what is happening and not perpetuate this unreasonable fear of color.

Rather than fear Black people's natural reaction of anger to the racism, it seems to me we should admire the fact that most African-Americans continue to try to love us in spite of our racist system. Do you think you would be able to even be civil, let alone friendly, to a group of people that regularly treated you as less than human?

African-Americans are largely angry at the system, not most white individuals. As some Blacks say, "There are `white people' and there are some people who happen to be white." Blacks are upset with "white people" who act as though their skin color makes them superior.

Most whites have been influenced negatively towards African-Americans by their families, peers and/or the media. Let's admit it and bring it out in the open so that we can begin to change and challenge our thinking and actions.

- **What does color matter? I don't look at color, only the person.**

- **If we all loved one another, we wouldn't have this problem, would we?**

Often whites, especially from a religious perspective, say they're not prejudiced because they don't see color; they just treat people as individuals. They say that color doesn't matter and that if we all loved one another, we would not have

30

a problem.

Well, if we're talking about the ideal, they may be right. However, if we only talk about how things should be and not how they are, we can never get things to where they could be.

As a woman, I would not expect a man to say my femininity does not matter, that he just sees me as another person. We also live in a sexist country and my being a female in a sexist system formed most of who I am and how I think and react. Not to take that into consideration is not to know me at all.

To ignore African-Americans' color is never to understand who they really are because color does matter in a racist system. Blacks are regularly treated differently because of their color. We don't all love each other, and until we admit how things really are, we can't change them.

CONCLUSION

White people seldom have to think about their color while African-Americans have to be aware of their color on a daily basis because they are daily treated differently because of it. It serves no purpose for whites to just relate to Blacks as though color didn't matter. Yes, we are all the same except for how we are treated based on color.

Too many whites act as though they're o.k. just because they know some Black people even though they usually don't really know the daily assaults that African-Americans put up with because of racism.

Though many Blacks try to maintain relationships with whites, they seldom fully share with them their experiences with white racism unless the whites make the first move to show that they are genuine, aware and want to know more.

African-Americans are not so much angry at individuals as they are with the system and the individuals who go along with the system that continues to persecute them.

"Most crime is Black on Black but when the victim is white, on the average, it is punished more severely."

A Common Destiny:
Blacks and American Society

Chapter 3

Crime

- **Why do Blacks kill each other?**

- **Why are there more crime and drugs in the Black community?**

Most of the crime in the Black community is committed by young Black males who have been left out of the mainstream with no hope for a future. They turn to crime and gangs as a way to survive in a system that offers no real alternatives. They may tell you that jail would be a step up. It may be the first time they ever have three meals a day, a stable roof over their heads and reliable medical care! Many Black children (males, especially) show signs of intellectual regression by fourth grade[3] because of the negative attitudes and treatment in the school system by white teachers, or by attending a predominantly Black school in an inner-city where the facilities, books, class size and conditions do not give them the opportunities to ever compete. Black males are singled out by racist teachers because they represent the biggest threat to white supremacy.

The research shows that aggression is a result of the social, psychological and economic conditions that result in overcrowding and poverty.[4] We also know that every percentage of unemployment causes an increase in murder,

33

suicide, crime and mental problems[5] no matter what color the people are. We said the same things about the Irish people when they first came here poor. They had gangs and more crime in their areas as well.

Most crime is Black on Black or white on white; however, when it is Black on white, it gets more media coverage and is more severely punished[6]. Most rapes are also Black on Black and white on white; however, when it is a Black man who rapes a white woman, he is more likely to get the death penalty, and no Black man has ever gotten the death penalty for raping a Black woman[7]. I'm pretty sure that the figures on rape do not reflect the numbers of Black women raped by white men (or Black men) because many Black women have shared with me that they did not bother to report their rapes because they felt that they would not be taken seriously.

Several white women who had been raped told me that when they reported the rape the first question the white police officers asked was, "What color was he?" If the woman said it was a Black man, the officer was very serious and supportive; whereas, when the woman said it was a white man who raped her, the officer seemed almost disappointed and showed little concern.

To be born a Black male in America is to be born a suspect. Few Black males, regardless of their education, escape from being pulled over by a police officer for no apparent reason and many are then spread-eagled on the car. A Black male has to be very careful how he moves or reaches for his license; the officer may think he's going for a gun to shoot him. Blacks are more likely to be arrested than whites, less likely to secure bail and more likely to serve the full term with no parole more than whites.[8]

Our justice system really only works for white people with money; poor people and people of color seldom get the same justice[9].

It's also important to remember the difficult position in which we put our police officers. Racism creates conditions where people are angry and have no reason to believe they will ever be able to compete so they do whatever they have to to survive; we expect the police officers to clean up this mess, to put their lives on the line everyday with little appreciation by Blacks or whites and we don't want to even know how they do it.

Remember, white police officers are also raised in a racist system that gives them negative attitudes about African-Americans and then when they largely deal with Blacks who are in trouble, it reinforces any stereotypes they may have. We also have stereotypes about white police officers; we often see them as brutal people who like to shoot and beat up people. If anyone should empathize with African-Americans, it should be police officers since they go through many of the isolating conditions that Blacks experience.

Most police officers are caring people, trying to do their job and help people. The problem is that we tend to blame them all when a few lose control. Often, through the "code of silence" that many police departments have, they are forced to be silent when they see another officer acting inappropriately. Some of the most sensitive men I have known from our seminars have been police officers; once you get to know them, you find that they have a lot of feelings and frustrations about their position. They are not used to being able to share that except in safe situations.

If we really want to reduce criminal activities to a manageable level, we need to eliminate the discrimination in all areas that keep African-Americans and many others from being gainfully employed. The relationship of employment to all other social conditions is undeniably at the heart of racist practices.

It's a lot less expensive to educate and train people and have them paying taxes than it is to keep them in jail later.

CONCLUSION

There is always more crime in areas where the people feel deprived and hopeless, no matter what color they are.

White to White on Black/White

African-Americans suffer more from the crime in their areas because crime naturally is more Black on Black and white on white; it's easier to commit crime where you don't stand out from the crowd. We also tend to let our frustrations out on the people closest to us.

As white people, we have an unreasonable fear of Blacks as criminals yet most crime done to us is by other whites. This means that the very people we ought to be more cautious of (whites), we do not worry much about and so put ourselves at risk.

People of any color who are left out will not have the same respect for life since life and death are much the same when you feel you have no future!

Chapter 4

Progress

- **Things are much better now; haven't we made progress?**

- **These things take time; why are Blacks so impatient?**

Most white Americans feel that America has made great progress in our treatment of African-Americans and that it will eventually be totally equal. They see changing the laws, so that it is illegal to discriminate, as major progress and seem to think things are gradually getting better.

While it is true that changing the laws to make sure all have equal opportunities is major progress, the problem is that we rarely enforce the laws and do not put anything in place in our education system to help the next generation eliminate their prejudicial attitudes. Our textbooks still hardly mention the contributions of people of color.

We have changed the areas that were obvious in terms of public accommodations but did not deal with the underlying problems of institutional racism.

We did begin to make progress after the Civil Rights Movement which resulted in changed laws, but since the late 1970's, things began to go backwards. The 1980's saw more Black families living in poverty and more Black children living under the poverty level than before the movement (45% Black, 39% Hispanic and 16% white).[10] The 1990 Census shows that   fewer   than   half   of   Black   males   had   full-time employment[11] and as high as 60% of young Black males (17-26) are unemployed in most of our major cities. College enrollment for Blacks dropped from 1976 to 1988 while for whites it increased. [12]

Living in poverty also decreases the quality of the education and health care people receive.[13] Many inner-city schools do not have the resources to provide a real education and Black babies still die twice as often as white babies in their first year of life. African-Americans have fifteen times more hypertension and related diseases than whites largely due to trying to survive in a racist system.[14]

If statistics showed that things were steadily moving forward for African-Americans, we could be more optimistic. However, the major statistics have gone all the way back to where they were before we changed the laws. Therefore, it doesn't make any sense to think that time will solve the problem unless we get serious about ways to stop the backslide.

We've really lost half of this generation of African-Americans and must get serious to save the next.

- **Blacks   are   natural   athletes   (or musicians), aren't they?**

- **Many Blacks are in high positions; doesn't that show progress?**

Another reason that white America thinks there is so much progress is that they see Black people at work who have important positions or famous Black athletes, actors, and musicians and even Blacks in high governmental positions. They don't see the 50% of Black males who have no future. They don't realize that the African-Americans they see are the

38

exception, not the rule. After all, most people are average and what happens to the average is what makes up America. There will always be the genius that you can't keep down no matter how many restrictions you place on them. How many white Americans are going to be Dr. J or Colin Powell?

Even in politics, the only real progress has been in the number of Black mayors and those are usually left in charge of cities that are more than 50% Black and have serious financial and social problems. African-Americans still only represent 1.5% of all elected officials.[15]

Whites also do not realize that most of the African-Americans who are employed, even at the higher level, still are impacted by racism daily. Black athletes and stars, in general, also do not get the same chance for endorsements and commercials that whites do nor the same chance to move into management.

African-Americans dominate athletics because it is one of the few areas that has allowed Blacks to compete equally and has rules that are enforced. So young Blacks work very hard at athletics because they see it as one of the few ways to be successful, and to get an education. It is very racist to say that Blacks are natural athletes as though it takes no brains, practice or effort. Most whites know there are other easier ways to achieve than athletics, therefore many don't put forth the same effort.

Much the same is true for the entertainment areas. Whites have always allowed Blacks to entertain them. The majority of our American music comes from Black musicians; even our country music was largely derived from Black's work songs during slavery. Jazz and Blues are the inventions of Black genius; most of America's music is derived from the foundation provided by Black artists, though most often they were not given the credit or recognition that they deserved.

- **I'm less prejudiced than my parents and I'm raising my children less prejudiced than I am; isn't prejudice getting less with each generation?**

- **Isn't it now a matter of economics and not race?**

White Americans often think that prejudice has diminished with each generation and so will eventually disappear. While it is probably true that people are less likely to see themselves as prejudiced now and that surveys show an improvement in white people's attitudes towards equal opportunity for Blacks,[16] they still resist any change that would affect them personally.

We also don't have to be as outright bigoted anymore - whites have developed a subtle system that does it very well for them. So even if you're really not prejudiced, chances are you're getting advantages from a system that is doing it for you!

African-American executives still face the "glass ceiling" that keeps them from moving beyond a certain level.[17] Our institutions have become more racist in such a subtle, complex way, that it is difficult to change even when we try.

Racism so pervades our society that recent studies show that by the age of four years, many white children already show signs of bigotry.[18] They see Black dolls as ugly, bad or dirty.

A few social scientists have talked about how race is less of an issue than it used to be - they say now it's more a matter of economics. More Black people are poor and so it is their economic status that keeps them deprived.

I would have to agree that living in poverty certainly changes most things about life, but if that was really the problem then middle-class and rich Blacks would not be facing racism daily. No matter how much money African-Americans have, they still face restrictions and rejection that whites do not. Money certainly makes it easier to shield oneself from some of the racism but certainly not from all of it. I know a few well-off Black male executives who won't even go to a grocery store in jeans because of the way they're treated (like a suspect)!

Also, when we try to say it's really economics and not race that accounts for the state that African-Americans are in, it really blames the victim. It does not take into consideration the racism that caused more Blacks to be economically deprived! There is something terribly wrong with our system if half the young Black males are unemployed - most people want to work, only 3-5% will be lazy. In America, we all start out wanting to be successful; no one starts out wanting to raise a family in a car or be a wino in America.

Blauner, in Black Lives, White Lives, concludes that "today the people left behind have less hope of a better life than in the sixties; the urban ghettos are even more economically and socially depressed and segregation - though no longer sanctioned by law - remains prevalent in schools and neighborhoods." [19]

Yes, changing our laws to give all equal rights was definite progress; public accommodations are now open and yet we're still very segregated and racism continues to limit African-Americans in countless and numerous ways.

CONCLUSION

At a time when most white Americans feel we have made great progress towards equal opportunities because of the legal changes and the achievement of some African-American exceptions, most African-Americans (even the middle-class and upper-class) feel that their children may have it worse because of the recession, lack of job opportunities and the rise of racism. For the most part, Americans are in denial of this gloomy prospect.

The recent riots are proof that many African-Americans

continue to be left out and have little reason to believe that they can achieve the all-American dream. People do not riot for an incident, as a rule. They have to be really angry, frustrated and feel that their lives are worth nothing to the system because of the years of incidents before rioting becomes an option.

Chapter 5

Innocence

- I didn't grow up with Blacks, I never met one until college; how could I be prejudiced?

Many whites do not grow up with any relationships with Blacks and it is not unusual for many whites to meet a Black person for the first time in college.

These real innocent whites never even thought about race relations although they may have seen TV programs dealing with the Black/white issue; it had no connection with their lives so it was easy to ignore. They also don't think of themselves as prejudiced towards Blacks but sometimes will be prejudiced toward another minority that was in their area (Native American, Hispanic, etc.).

There also are some whites who grew up with Blacks in a very mixed area where everyone got along and may not realize until they move away that this is a real exception.

The person who is really innocent will be shocked and surprised to find out how much racism there is in every facet of American life and also is more likely to try to make up for this lost time. They often read everything they can find on the issue and are enthusiastic about sharing their new learning with anyone who will listen. It's also important to note that all white people who say they're innocent are really not innocent;

they only know enough to be dangerous! The people who are pretending to be innocent are easy to spot because when you try to give them information, they usually will argue with you. They'll talk about some article they read or some statistic they heard. Anytime people know enough to argue with you, they're not as innocent as they would have you believe.

I think that people pretending to be innocent are also largely the reason that many African-Americans gave up even trying to share their feelings and experiences with whites. These people often ask questions of Blacks that show they're not really serious. They ask things like "What do you Black people want, anyhow?" or "How does it feel to be Black in America?"

These are questions we can answer for ourselves. We do not need to ask Blacks. All we have to do is to ask ourselves "How would I feel if I was treated differently daily because of my color?" "What would I want under those conditions?"

Black people feel the same as we do when we're mistreated or prejudged because it is a human response. We may not be able to understand totally the depth of what African-Americans experience but we know for sure if we were treated that way, we'd want it to stop; we know it is very painful to be rejected and that it has many psychological consequences.

Once we've figured out the basic questions for ourselves, then the questions we have are more serious and I've found that most African-Americans are very willing to share with white people who are serious. People automatically don't share their painful experiences with people who don't give them some reason to believe that they could understand. African-Americans also don't share until they find out "Where you're coming from" and what you're likely to do with the information. Too often when they have shared, it was used against them. There is no reason for whites to stay innocent. The information is out there if we want to know.

The fact that whites can grow up not knowing about the racism is a reflection and confirmation of our institutional racism. If we were educated truthfully about our past instead of distorting it, we would understand the system of white privilege and Black oppression.

It's been my experience that it's hard to live with yourself knowing that you are part of a problem (racism) that destroys a large segment of our population and puts us all in jeopardy of losing our freedom and democracy. Once you really understand the devastation of racism, you want to become a part of the solution.

- **I grew up in the North where there wasn't so much prejudice; the South is where the real bigots are, right?**

There is a tendency for white people who grow up in the North to think that the real bigots are in the South.

Though there are differences in how racism has been acted out North and South, all parts of American Society are racist, regardless of the area.[20]

The North has often been more subtle in its expressions of racism and appears more open than it really is. We saw what happened when the northern schools tried to integrate; the same old hatred and bigotry came out. We often did not realize how much was there until it became a community issue.

In the South, racism was acted out more openly by having signs that made it clear where Black people belonged. It was difficult for southern whites to say they didn't know what was happening.

The out-front mistreatment of Blacks caused southern whites to have to make a decision: They either decided that this was no way to treat human beings and stood up against it or if they were going to allow this mistreatment, they had to rationalize it in order to still feel good about themselves. Sadly, the church often gave them a rationalization by saying that Blacks did not have a soul and were more like animals.

In the South, you have what I call "good bigots"; at least they will argue with you as to why they were that way and why they wanted to stay that way. In the North, most of us ended up prejudiced without having to even think about it or admit it to ourselves. So when we see racism acted out openly, we see it as worse.

Now that the South has major companies in most large urban areas and Blacks and whites are working together in a whole new way, it looks like the South has made serious progress. However, I'm afraid much of the progress is just a matter of whites learning to "tolerate" Blacks rather than totally accepting them. I would never use the word tolerate in relationship with human beings. Tolerate is to "put up with". Human beings are to be accepted and appreciated for their uniqueness, not tolerated. It used to be that Blacks knew whom they could trust when racism was out in the open. Now, it works in all parts of the country more like the Northern version.

At work, people tolerate each other and make the normal small talk about their work, sports, and families, but African-Americans tell me that many of these same people who seem so nice at work won't speak to them when they're away from work. It's hard to know who you can really trust under those conditions.

Also, in the South, when you leave the major urban areas, many places are just like the old days. There are serious Ku Klux Klan areas that you better not have to stop in if you're Black. In those areas, racism is still practiced more openly.

The hate groups are not limited to the South; they are all over America and some fourteen new groups have appeared in the past decade. Their belief in white supremacy is built around a "theology" that says whites are God's chosen people and people of color and Jewish people are less, that they come from the devil.

White supremacists thrive during times when jobs are scarce because they blame Blacks for taking "their" jobs. They also have a political strategy to elect people who support their ideology. They may still be a small group in America but they will speak for us if we are passive or ignorant of their plans.

Innocence

- ## Children don't see color so if I don't mention it, they'll be unprejudiced, won't they?

Rarely do white parents tell their children to be prejudiced against people of color. In fact, in most cases parents don't talk about it at all. Parents think that if they don't tell their children about prejudice, they won't be prejudiced.

Unfortunately, in America, white children are taught to be sexist and racist everyday by the culture; if their parents don't do something on a continual basis to counteract it, the children will become part of the problem.

Television continues to give us stereotyped views of people of color in many subtle (and some not so subtle) ways. Parents, often unconsciously, give their children clues to their covert racist beliefs by such things as only locking their car doors when they're in a Black area, being more protective of their children when near Blacks and even by not having any Black friends at their home.

Little children are very observant; they're continually trying to figure out the norms and they pay very close attention to all things and people they see.

When they go to school, they are taught history in a way that excludes most people of color in a positive way and makes it look like white people are the only ones who ever did anything worthwhile. They leave out the tremendous contributions of African-Americans that have helped America prosper. This gives white children an unconscious feeling of being better than people of color.

Our schools do not teach the real history of white racism in America or the struggles that African-Americans have gone through because of it. Until we are honest with our children about the destruction that white people have perpetuated (such as taking land from the Native Americans, making treaties that were never kept and putting small pox in peace blankets; the horrors of slavery which made Black human beings property

47

with no rights or protection) all children grow up with a false sense of who they really are in connection with the whole.

CONCLUSION

White people know little about how racism operates, and about the daily impacts it has on African-Americans.

There are many white people who did not grow up ever seeing Blacks and are very ignorant of the problem of racism and there also are whites who pretend like they want to know but whose questions make it clear they prefer not to really know enough to have to act on the problem.

Whites also tend to think that Southerners are the real bigots because they do not see how Northerners practice racism in more subtle ways. Neither the North nor the South ever allowed Black people to be full human beings in the American society.

Whites also think their children will not be prejudiced if they don't tell them about it, while the media and the culture continues to make our children racist and sexist.

Chapter 6

Passivity

- **I never did anything to Blacks, do I have
  to be responsible for our ancestors?**

Sometimes white people don't see it as their responsibility to do anything about racism. They say they're not doing anything to anyone and that they can't be held responsible for what their ancestors did.

While it may be true that we can't change the past, we do have a responsibility to change the present. Racism is destroying people <u>now</u> and continues to give white people advantages and opportunities that keeps them from competing fairly with all Americans.

As long as we are participating in a system that does it for us, without trying to change it, we are very much a part of the problem. Could you run a race against someone who had a broken leg and feel good about winning? Could you even call it a race?

- **Whites are prejudiced but so are Blacks,
  isn't everyone?**

Another way that whites justify not doing anything about

prejudice is by saying that we're all prejudiced and that Blacks are racist against whites, too.

It's true that most African-Americans have anger and hostility towards the white system that discriminates against them and treats them as less than human beings. That's not prejudiced or racist; it's a natural reaction to mistreatment. Blacks are not prejudging whites; they have good reasons based on years of negative experiences.

White people can't name anything that Blacks have done to whites as a group that is not a reaction to racism nor can most whites name anything that has been done to them on an individual basis. Even if they had a bad personal experience, it would not make them prejudiced to whites in general if it was a white person who mistreated them. When whites have a bad experience with Black people, it reinforces their stereotypes and they do not see it as an indivdiual experience.

Most African-Americans are taught to treat white people with respect as well as how to cope with white people who do not treat them as full human beings.

I've been the only white person in many all Black groups and was made to feel comfortable and welcome by most. The treatment I've received in Black churches has been especially wonderful. It seems to me that African-Americans go out of their way to prove that they're accepting of everyone who shows an effort.

On the other hand, they would be crazy to trust whites just because we show up. When you're done in on a regular basis, you naturally reserve a part of yourself until you are sure you can trust.

- **I don't have a problem with Blacks but why should I suffer with property values going down when they move in?**

- **Why should I challenge a racist; we all have a right to our opinion, don't we?**

Passivity

- **I don't have a problem with Blacks and whites marrying but how would I deal with my family and friends who do?**

Though many white Americans don't think of themselves as racists, they also remain part of the problem because of their passivity. Since it doesn't hurt them directly, it is easy to ignore situations.

There is a tendency to conform to how things are rather than to challenge them. When you're in an environment that supports prejudice it seems easier and more profitable to go along. Many people feel that they will be ostracized by their friends and families if they speak up.

What do you feel when you hear outright bigotry? Do you feel ashamed, embarrassed or guilty? Or do you feel outrage, anger and disgust? Are you moved to action?

Embarrassment, shame and guilt are passive feelings and make you less likely to respond, while anger, outrage and disgust are more likely to make you active. Passive feelings are a result of knowing on some level that you are part of the problem and those passive feelings go away when you decide to be part of the solution.

Everybody may have a right to their opinion but we also have a responsibility to challenge that opinion when people are being destroyed by it.

Many people who consider themselves Christians also are so busy trying to be nice and loving that they end up being passive. They don't allow themselves to get upset enough to do anything. They need to be reminded that Jesus was not passive; Jesus acted when he saw injustice.

Religious people are the largest group we have in America who believe we're all created equally and that we should all love one another. If we could just get them to be active on racism, perhaps we could solve the problem.

During the Civil Rights Movement, religious people became involved because they understood that racism goes against the basic theme of religion which is to love one another. Most ministers were educating their congregations in the 60's to the issues. Reactivating religious people will be an important part of the solution in eliminating racism in America.

White people often say that it doesn't bother them if African-Americans live in their neighborhood or socialize with whites but the peer pressure of other whites keeps them from saying anything. Property Values do not go down because Blacks move in. They go down because whites panic and move out. When someone tells a racial joke at a party; whites who don't like it may walk away but they won't express their disapproval. It's been my experience that when someone does speak up and say the joke is offensive, at least half of the people will agree that they didn't like it either.

So our passivity is allowing the serious racists (who are in the minority) to control what is acceptable for the rest of us. To be silent is to condone racist behavior. It causes us to lose the precious freedom that we say is so important to a democracy. If whites began to express their opinions against racism, we could turn the peer pressure around and make the racist unacceptable. That would allow us to really live up to our stated values of liberty and justice for all.

CONCLUSION

White Americans have a tendency to remain part of the problem of racism because of their passivity. We find excuses to balance our prejudice with Blacks' reaction against racism and to find a way to rationalize our passivity.

We're allowing the bigots to control America though they are in the minority; many whites who say they are all for the rights of African-Americans are not willing to speak up or vote for the necessary changes to make America less racist. So they continue to be part of the problem through their passivity and the disease of racism continues. Change requires action, not passivity.

"Keys to eliminating racism are held by the racists, not the victims."

Impacts of Racism on White Americans

"Black and white educational opportunities are not equal. Standards of academic performance for teachers and students are not equivalent to whites in predominantly Black schools."

Common Destiny: Blacks and American Society

Chapter 7

Bootstraps

- Why don't Blacks work as hard as we do?

- Why don't Blacks take advantage of the opportunities out there?

- If Blacks would just get more education, that would eventually solve the problem, wouldn't it?

White people often think that African-Americans don't work as hard as they do and feel that there are many opportunities available to Blacks if they would take advantage of them. We act as though getting an education solves all the problems.

Many whites came from poverty conditions and worked their way up and don't understand why others can't do the same thing.

The truth is that no one works harder for just an existence than poor people. If hard work was all it took, we wouldn't have so many poor white people in America.

We often don't consider the psychological consequences of being poor. At least for us as whites, we had some reason to believe that if we worked hard and got an education, we could achieve some level of success. We live in a country where we have been given images of white people who have come from poverty and achieved great success. We were told and shown that "even a poor boy could become President."

African-American children knew that we really meant a poor, white boy could be President, and as a woman I knew that a white girl could maybe be First Lady but not President. Maybe this generation of women can begin to think a woman could be President but it never occurred to me when I was growing up! We tend to aspire to what seems possible.

We haven't given Black children the same reason to believe that Blacks can achieve in any but the rarest cases. Many African-Americans have achieved miraculously in spite of poverty and racism but we never included them in our history or put their images out there for Black children to see.

We still have not included people of color in our American history; most schools only have a little Black History once a year. I know a white teacher that told her class that they would be talking about Black History tomorrow and that the Black children did not have to come to class if it would embarrass them!! Obviously, she didn't even know Black History and was going to focus on slavery, not the struggles and accomplishments Blacks made in spite of it!

So Black children growing up in poverty don't have much reason to believe that anything they do will make a difference. Some of the people they see who did get an education are still doing janitor jobs. They don't see why you have to go to college for that job level. Even when Black males have a college education, they only make as much money as a white male high school graduate. Even Black males with graduate degrees, on the average, make less than white males with a graduate degree but also make about the same as a Black male high school graduate.[21] It would appear that the more education the Black man has, the more of a threat he is.

In spite of the lack of reason to believe education will allow one to achieve, in the past African-Americans were making great progress in education; however, in the 1980's when financial aid was cut and tuition continued to rise, Blacks were the first ones to feel the crunch; Hispanics also were likely to feel there was no way they could go to college; even middle-class whites now are in a panic about how they will be able to get their children through college.

If all you can get is a minimum wage job, you'll be lucky to pay personal expenses and books, let alone tuition and room and board! It's not as possible to work your way through college as it was twenty years ago.

Most poor African-American children growing up in the inner cities have little reason to believe they can ever go to college. Many of the inner-cities' schools have such a poor level of education that even if students graduate, they don't have enough education to compete on a college level.

The conditions in many inner-city schools are so disgusting and hopeless that any education that takes place is a miracle. There are schools where the sewage backs up in the restrooms, where the ground is saturated with toxic waste and where there are not enough textbooks or lab supplies for all students to have them. (Read Savage Inequalities by Jonathon Kozol - see reading list for details). Any child growing up in this generation that does not have access to computers will also be at a serious disadvantage for the future workforce.

The very least we need to do in America is to make sure that all of our children have access to the same education regardless of their socio-economic status. If we don't provide education and training for poor children, we will pay for it on the other end.

Since there are few training programs for the new, more skilled jobs, many inner-city youths feel like their only options are to take a fast-food job with no health benefits or to sell drugs. That's not much of a choice and when the only people they see having anything nice are those who are dealing drugs, they are more than tempted. They don't want to be a drain on their families; they want to contribute. No one starts out wanting to be a nobody; there's something terribly wrong with our system if every other young Black male is unemployed. People will find a way to survive but it usually isn't a way we would approve.

White to White on Black/White

In spite of the difficulties, many African-Americans do complete a college education but find they cannot get a job that utilizes their education. In the 1990's, a bachelor's degree doesn't mean what it used to. White graduates also are likely to have to start at a lower level than they thought they would with a college education.

Even when Black students get an entry level job, they seldom move up at the same pace as whites do. I meet Blacks all the time who have masters degrees and are working at high school level jobs. America is losing because we do not use the abilities of our minority citizens. We've proven that discrimination still plays a large part in the unemployment and under-employment of Blacks and it is a well-known fact in Black families that you have to work twice as hard to get half as far. There is a real discrepancy in promotions and most all Blacks that get to be in charge of others have more education and experience than most whites in the same position.

For many Blacks, there is not much motivation to work hard. When you're in a dead-end job with no hope of moving up, no one works as hard, regardless of their color.

-   **Why are so many Blacks on welfare?**

-   **Why do young Black women have babies when they're unmarried?**

The media gives us the feeling that Blacks are the major recipients of welfare when in terms of numbers, there are more whites on welfare. The whole Welfare System only encourages people to remain on it. It penalizes people for any progress they might make. It causes fathers to leave home in order for their children to get aid.

You can't afford to work at a minimum wage job with no health benefits if you have children and when you also have to pay for day care, transportation and clothes, you end up in "the hole".

Sure, there will always be people who are lazy but most people want to work and provide for themselves and feel like their work will be rewarded.

We also talk about Black women having babies just to get more welfare money. Anyone who has a child knows that's not realistic; you only get $2.50 - $3.00 a day for a child; you're lucky to feed them on that amount. Research shows that there is no evidence that welfare aid for dependent children is an incentive to have babies.[22] The yearly average amount that welfare mothers receive is $2,995.00.[23] Poor people usually have more children than others. They have less access to birth control information and more of a need to prove they can do something special. Having a baby is an accomplishment and it makes you special in a world that looks down on you. Unmarried, young, Black women are less likely to abort their babies, as well.[24] Having a baby can also be a positive motivator to struggle to overcome the poverty and racism.

Remember that most of the negative stereotypes we have of Blacks in America are the same things that many poor people do. We keep expecting people to have middle class values and lifestyles who are struggling just to survive. Most Black families have values that are similar to most white families in the same socio-economic class and in many cases, better values in terms of how they treat people. The media largely focuses on the negatives that reinforce stereotypes.

Most of the money spent on welfare in America goes to the people who administer it, not to the people who need it! In New York City in 1983, only 37% went to poor people. [25]

The number of children growing up in America under the poverty level is a disgrace. We have 45% of the Black children, 39% of Hispanic children and 16% of white children living below the poverty level;[26] they will be less likely to ever become a productive part of America. Without proper care, nutrition and education, they will return to haunt us. We are just blaming the victims and perpetuating the cycle of poverty.

- **Other minorities and immigrants have made it; why can't Blacks?**

America is a nation of immigrants and it seems to me that we should have more empathy for people who are struggling. Most of our ancestors came here poor and were mistreated the first or second generations because of their different customs and language. Once they were accepted, they were expected to be against the other groups who were not.

Sure, our immigrant ancestors worked hard and often were made to feel so ashamed of their backgrounds that they changed their names to better fit into society. There were also more opportunities for unskilled labor than we have now. These ethnic groups also most often had a family support system that allowed them to feel good about themselves. Racism makes it more difficult to keep a family intact.

When we took in the Vietnamese refugees, we provided some support for them. Our churches sponsored families to help them get established. Yes, they did work hard as well and most Asian immigrants come here with a willingness to work harder than most of us who were born here.

Remember, in America the research shows that the level of your success is controlled by your color.[27] The more color you have, the more discrimination you're likely to face and if you are white your color gives you an advantage over people of color.

So, African-Americans have all the same problems that white people do plus the disadvantage that racism adds. Think how difficult it would be to keep your children feeling good about themselves when they are continually being treated as less than human by so many white people. One young African-American woman told me how hurt and devastated she was at the age of eight when she first realized that whites treated her more like an animal than a human being. Another shared how frightened she was in elementary school when some white children painted a Barbie Doll black, put a rope around its neck, and hung it in her locker. I know as a mother that it takes a lot of work to build back a child's self-esteem when just one negative thing is said to her by one teacher.

It's clear to me that the strength and support that African-American parents have to provide for their children is on a level that most white parents do not know. I'm sure that white parents of children who are physically or mentally challenged understand better what regular put-downs can do. Think how much more difficult it would be to add color to also being physically or mentally challenged.

I've always been impressed how many African-Americans that I've met have survived the assaults of whites with a good sense of themselves; however it's harder to face up to how many Black children have been destroyed psychologically from the racism they faced.

CONCLUSION

White people have a tendency to compare African-Americans' lack of progress and poverty conditions to poor whites, other minorities and immigrants who have made it. We blame them for not taking advantage of opportunities because we don't want to admit the part that racism plays in the lives of Black people. We act as though whites achieve because they work hard while ignoring the fact that the hardest working people America ever had were slaves. If hard work was all it took, African-Americans would be on top. Racism kept them from being in full competition with whites and so kept them from ever reaping the rewards from their hard work.

Racism puts Black people in a position where they have to be super-human to survive and then blames those that don't as though things were equal.

"...so sexuality and racism must be indeed intertwined."

White Racism: A Psycho History

Chapter 8

Interracial Marriage - Sex

- The Bible says the races should not mix; we can be fair without intermarriage, can't we?

- Haven't studies shown that Blacks have lower I.Q.'s than whites?

- Kind should stick to kind, shouldn't they?

- If Blacks and whites have babies together, they come out white on one side and black on the other, (or mottled skin), don't they?

Most white Americans now will agree that African-Americans should be able to have equal opportunities for jobs, housing, schools and social activities.   So why does discrimination continue despite our changed laws and attitudes? Racism continues because even most liberal white people have some problems when it comes to their own children being involved sexually with the Black race, especially interracial marriage.

If we truly had equal opportunities in all the other areas,

63

the interaction would result in Black Americans becoming part of our families and most whites have problems with that.

Gunner Mrydal in the American Dilemma shows that white Americans fear Blacks marrying into the family, socializing with Blacks, living in the same neighborhoods with Blacks, going to school with Blacks and working with Blacks, in that order.[28] Notice that the closer the personal contact becomes, the higher the fear is on the list.

So even though we say African-Americans should have equal opportunity, we do everything possible to make sure that we have as little interaction as possible.

The most blatant racists will tell us that the races should not mix, that the Bible says we should not mix, that kind should stick to kind, that Blacks have lower I.Q.'s and that the mixed children will come out either white on one side and Black on the other or have mottled skin (dark with big white spots).

This whole line of reasoning leads to the conclusion, either consciously or unconsciously, that Black people are not full human beings, that they are more like animals!

It makes no biological or logical sense that God does not want the races to mix! The people in the Bible were people of color (most whites think they were all white and spoke English). Moses was married to a Black woman and Jesus' lineage included many races. People also say that bluebirds and robins don't mix so Black and white people should not mix! It seems to me that if God did not want us together, God would not have made it possible; bluebirds and robins can't reproduce together - all colors of people can!

I think the concept of "kind should stick to kind" is an important concept; the problem is the interpretation of "kind". If my daughter tells me she wants to marry a horse, I'll be upset - that is not her kind! However, if she wants to marry a human being, that is her kind! Human beings and animals should not be trying to reproduce together; that's what "kind should stick to kind" means, not one's color!

In the past, there was an attempt to prove that Blacks were less evolved and had lower I.Q.'s than white people but the only thing that was ever proven is that living in poverty conditions means that you don't score as high on tests that were designed for middle-class white children! It also does not test a child's ability to achieve in school when given the same opportunity as others.

As far as interracial children coming out with skin that is white on one side and black on the other or with spots, that is too ludicrous for any thinking person to ever verbalize! Eighty per cent of Blacks in America are already part white and some of the most beautiful people are racially mixed. We make beautiful babies Black and white and those are the ones white people will elect as Miss America! As white people, we know that having color makes you prettier! We're the only people who spend humongous amounts of time and money just to darken our natural color so we'll look better.

We also say that Black is dominant so that eventually white people will disappear; however, given the small percentage of Blacks in America (12 - 15%) and the fact that 80% of them are already part white, it would not take long for them to be the ones to disappear if there was serious interracial marriage. White people might get a little more melanin (color) to help protect them from skin cancer!

There is no such thing as keeping the race "pure", especially in America - we're very much already mixed! I know many white people who look just like Black people I know! I know Black people who look like most white people. If it wasn't for racism, we all could be proud to acknowledge our multi-cultural racial heritage.

Remember, in America, if you have any "Black" in you, you're technically considered to be Black, whether it shows or not.

- **The children of an interracial marriage suffer; why put them through pain?**

White to White on Black/White

- **Why would I want my children to marry a Black since it would cause extra problems?**

For those white Americans who know there is no reason based on the Bible or physical consequences for Blacks and whites not to be together, they justify their attitudes by talking about the extra problems an interracial couple will have or how the interracial children suffer and are not accepted by Blacks or whites.

When we talk about interracial children suffering, it's clear to me that this is more of an excuse! If we cared about children suffering, we would get rid of racism, which destroys children everyday. We would not care only when they're going to be in our family!

It's also true that interracial children often have it a little easier than most Blacks in America since the lighter you are the more acceptable you are to white people and also if you have a white side of the family, it could make it possible to have some inroads to the white system most Blacks would not have.

The interracial children who really suffer (remember, most of the Blacks in America are already interracial though whites do not see them as such for the most part) are those who have either been raised by white parents in an all-white situation with no reality given to their Blackness or those raised by a Black/white couple trying to pretend that racism does not exist!

I've had white mothers with Black children tell me that they explained the child's color by saying that "Mommy is white, Daddy is Black and so you're tan."!! I've even had a divorced white mother tell me in our seminars that her child is so light they never told her she is part Black!

These parents are setting their children up to be psychologically disturbed and devastated when they find out how white Americans will treat them when they go out in the real, racist world!

Interracial Marriage - Sex

While I can understand the parents wanting their children to appreciate their white part, it is unrealistic not to teach them to be very proud of their Black part since that's what America will focus on!

It's not true that interracial children are not accepted by the African-American community. Most Blacks in America are already interracial and many have white people in their extended families - to not accept interracial children is to not accept themselves. However, Blacks will have problems with the interracial children who have been raised to deny the Black part of their heritage, do not yet understand what it means to be Black in America or act as though they're better than other Blacks.

Also remember that American racism depends on all the minority groups hating each other and that it also creates many divisions among each minority to make them fuss with each other because it takes the focus off the real problem of white racism. A racist system may treat a light-Black person better but it does not totally accept them either. Most Black people know this and some of the most serious African-Americans that I know in fighting racism are light-skinned Blacks.

The other concern white Americans have about their children marrying interracially is that white society does not really accept interracial marriages and that they don't want their children to have any extra problems since marriage already ends in divorce half the time in America.

Being a mother of four myself, I certainly can understand not wanting your children to have to suffer any more than necessary; however, I also know it's really not my choice to decide whom they marry. If white society will give them problems, then my only choice is to try to change the attitudes that would cause them problems so that they can be free to really have a choice. I refuse to limit my children; I want them to have the world to choose from, not just one small part!

It seems to me that if we really care about our children, we would only be concerned about the character of the person they want to marry, not the color. Actually, the studies show that a Black/white marriage (if it survives the initial problems of the first two years) has a better chance to last forever than a white/white or Black/Black marriage. You have to be more serious in your love and commitment to marry interracially because society will not allow you to ignore the differences.

-   **Blacks don't want interracial marriage either, do they?**

-   **Black men want to marry white women as a way of improving their status, don't they?**

-   **Black men want to go with white women as revenge against white men, don't they?**

-   **What would a Black and white see in each other; why would they date?**

There are a lot of theories and discussions about why Blacks and whites choose to be together and how African-Americans don't want interracial marriage either.

We talk about how Blacks just marry whites to improve their social status, how Black men "take" white women as their revenge on white men and how the whites involved are seen as lower level (trashy) people.

While a racist society does create certain psychological problems for both Blacks and whites, the majority of people who intermarry do not do it because of the reasons we talk about. Most interracial couples get married because they met and really liked each other just like most other couples!

There are many interracial marriages among celebrities because they are in close contact with each other and can protect themselves from many of the problems the average person faces.

Many of the interracial marriages between white women

and Black men are with white women who have been divorced from oppressive or abusive white men and have an automatic empathy with Black men who are also under the oppressive white male system. It's often easier to have an equal relationship with a Black male and more chance for a white woman to really share her feelings with a Black male since he has similar experiences and feelings.

The surveys show that African-Americans accept interracial marriages in general and that most interracial couples live in the Black community. However, we often hear hostility coming from Blacks without understanding what they're upset about. Most all complaints we hear from African-Americans about interracial marriage are a direct reaction to a racist system.

We most often hear hostility to an interracial couple by single Black women because they are the ones most left out. The number of eligible Black men to marry is limited due to the large number of Black men who are unable to get a job with any future for supporting a family. White men are not lining up to marry Black women in any numbers. So, when a Black woman sees a white woman with a Black man, her first reaction may well be "Darn, there goes another one!" Of course, we white women aren't stupid either; we want a guy with a good job, too! It's been my experience that once a Black woman sees that the white woman and the Black man have a serious relationship going, she accepts it. She does not really care if Black and white people get married to each other; she already knows and accepts that in her own family. What she does care about is that it's not a two-way street and that racism is limiting her chances (and her children's) for finding a man with whom she can share her life.

It's also easy to understand a Black father's initial concern for his daughter going out with a white guy. Fathers, in general, are very protective of their daughters so when you add race to it, it is more difficult. Since white men have a long history of just using Black women, the Black father has to make sure the white guy who wants to date his daughter is going to not only treat her right but also will have enough courage to protect her from any racist whites they might encounter.

Black parents also have to worry about what might happen to their son if he dates a white woman. We have enough instances of interracial couples being mistreated or even shot in America to have to worry about a son's safety when he's with a white woman.

It also seems logical to me that Black mothers might prefer that their sons marry Black women since they know there are few eligible men from which Black women can choose.

Of course, you're also going to always have a few African-Americans who have experienced such mistreatment and oppression from whites that they don't want anything to do with their oppressors.

Basically, African-Americans are taught to love and accept all people and know that no race is more superior than another (although Blacks have shown they are superior in terms of continuing to teach love under the difficult system of racism and are far more accepting of others than are whites).

- **Is it true that Black men are better (or bigger) in bed?**

- **When white women go with Black men, they never go back to white men, do they?**

Though most white Americans do not want any of their children to marry Blacks, the real fear is the Black male and the white female. This is the combination that causes many white males to get upset.

Black males are the group that is the most threatening to a system of white male supremacy and thus are the target of the most blatant racism in an attempt to make Black men frightening and unappealing to white women. We have created myths and stereotypes about Black males to further this purpose.

We begin to see that racism and sexism are very much connected because they are both an attempt by white males to own and control others. In the days of slavery, white men did as they pleased with Black women (that's part of the reason most Blacks in America are part white) and they wanted to make sure white women did not get together with Black men.

Remember, in those days the white woman was put on a pedestal and protected since she was seen as fragile, culturally naive and easily seduced. She wasn't even supposed to like sex; she only endured it as her wifely duty! No wonder many white men went elsewhere for sex. White men with money often had a Black mistress on the side with whom he fathered children. Thomas Jefferson had children with his Black mistress and even moved her into his home after his wife died. In some cases, these white men really took care of their Black families and started Black colleges as a way of getting their Black offspring educated. They left them land or money in their wills.

The white wives of these men were supposed to be too naive to notice that their husbands had another family. White women were told that Black men were animalistic, heavy-hung and over-sexed as a way of scaring them. There were laws on the books like "reckless eye-balling" which said if a Black man was caught even looking at a white woman, he could be beaten or lynched.

White and Black children often grew up together and were friends (especially in the South) as children. However, as puberty approached, those friendships were discouraged and cut off by the white parents. Eventually, Black parents were forced to prepare their children for the end of these friendships to lessen the pain of rejection.

The same system is still in place today in most white people's unconsciousness; it's done to us more subtlely.

The real difference today is that being sexual is a positive thing and the stereotypes we put on the Black male about being bigger and better in bed makes white males feel insecure since they can't compete with the stereotype. These stereotypes and myths are largely humorous to white women; we wonder why men think that sex is another competitive sport where the biggest one wins? We went through a phase in America where women tried to treat men as sex objects but it did not last long because most of us are looking for a person we can really share ourselves with, not just someone which whom we can have sex.

Women don't love men for their organs; I often say that when we're totally honest with ourselves, sometimes we love them in spite of their organs. Sex is only a small part of a real relationship, not the only part.

We also say Black men have more endurance and can "go all night". That's the least of our worries - Americans are the busiest people I know! We all have to work tomorrow; who has time to go all night? It will be a rare occasion when we have the time, inclination or energy!

So men, if you're trying to impress women, get a tear in your eye, be sensitive to our feelings and share your feelings with us, and forget about size and time. It's the attitude that you make love with, not the equipment, that is the most important.

I know there are some Black males (especially young) who try to pretend that the stereotype is real but who can blame them for that? It's the only thing we give them credit for; it's the only way we allow young Black males to be fully men.

White women and white men also have different reasons for their reactions to interracial marriage, in most cases. A white male most often has a "gut" reaction to seeing a white woman with a Black man. He can't usually even articulate it, let alone explain it. He can't come up with any real reason that makes sense and so will start making excuses like they'll have more problems and the grandchildren will suffer. In most cases, it is an emotional reaction, not a rational one for white men.

On the other hand, white women, for the most part, do not have the emotional reaction to an interracial couple - we're more likely to smile and say to ourselves "they look so sweet in love." If it were up to white women, this sexual hang-up that discourages interracial marriage would be gone.

What happens to most of us as white women is the peer pressure that causes us to go along with the system. By the time we're teens, most of us know that if we date a Black guy, no white guy will go out with us. While there are white guys who would still date us, we were led to believe we'd be totally ostracized. So white women have gone along with the white male system and allowed ourselves to be owned and used in the process - largely without realizing it. Our real concern is the peer pressure, and how white males will view our daughters if they choose to date a Black man.

Fortunately, younger liberated white women are more aware that white men often view them as a piece of property and that they can tell them what to do and whom they should date (owned?). Many younger white women are not putting up with the peer pressure that causes them to feel owned and limited in quite the same way. They are trying to make their own choices.

I personally feel that as white women we also have the responsibility of being more open and honest with white men on how it makes us feel to be considered a piece of property, owned, and used to keep racism going.

As white women, we often blame white males for all the problems - the 1990's truly have begun as a decade of verbal "White male-bashing". It seems to me that as white women we also have to face our role in this racist system. White women raised those white males to fit into a sexist, racist culture and got the benefits and advantages from the system that did it for them. They helped keep the separation going.

I see many white men trying to be less racist and sexist but women often don't appreciate their struggle and give them so many mixed signals that white men end up very frustrated and put down. If we really want our country to eliminate racism and sexism, it will be necessary for men and women and Blacks and whites to be more honest with each other and work out our problems together.

CONCLUSION

Sexual racism is the main reason that we have not been able to rid our system of discrimination against African-Americans.

If we really considered African-Americans as full human beings, we would not even be questioning whether they can be in our schools, neighborhoods or families.

White people will say they're not prejudiced, that they just "prefer" whites to marry. Clearly, to me, one has to be taught to write off a whole group of people you haven't even met yet! It really shows the power of a racist system when you can subconsciously be convinced that you're not attracted to any person of a certain group! Opposites often do attract and it takes a lot of conditioning to keep people apart.

We continue to pass racism on to the next generation for no good reason, because it is easier to go along with the system. We are taking away the freedom of our children to make their own choices and making color more important than character.

We also know that we're going to have to be there for our children when they do marry, no matter who they marry; so let's quit passing down these limitations that cause us all more problems than they solve.

Chapter 9

Affirmative Action

- Blacks are taking our jobs.

- Affirmative Action makes white people resentful; why do we still need it?

When white people in America complain that African-Americans are taking their jobs, it shows how much we are taught to think racist. Black people are Americans too; they have just as much right to the jobs as whites do! In fact, most African-Americans have been here longer than most European-Americans.

The problem with employment in America in the 1990's is that we don't have enough jobs for all the people who want to work. When jobs are scarce, whites feel threatened because they are used to having the advantage of being considered first by most employers for the jobs. Any extra competition is amplified in tough economic times.

Obviously, whites don't normally think about the advantage they have. I remember when I first realized that it was not just my hard work that allowed me to be successful; someone took away part of my competition. I did not ask them to do that; I would much prefer to achieve on my own merits. As white people, we can never know if we would achieve at the same level if we really had to compete with

75

everyone and African-Americans can never know what they might have been had they had equal opportunities.

Affirmative Action was supposed to get employers to consider the people they had ignored in the past so that we could utilize everyone's talents. If Affirmative Action really worked the way many whites think it has, we wouldn't have half of young, Black males unemployed or half of Black children growing up in poverty. White women have probably gained the most from Affirmative Action in terms of wages and positions though there is still discrimination against them.

It would also appear that Affirmative Action will be the least of our concerns for the future. The new figures for the year 2000 show that the <u>new</u> workforce will be composed of only 15% white males. The majority will consist of women and minorities of color.[29] If we don't fully use the talents and skills of all our citizens, we won't have enough workers to economically compete in the world. We've already lost an estimated 105 billion dollars a year in gross national product because of discrimination.[30] We must concentrate on job creation and making sure that this generation gets educated and trained for the jobs of the future or we all lose.

- **Quotas are not fair; why can't we just hire the most qualified?**

- **Why should we not just accept students with the best grades into medical schools (or colleges)?**

- **Why should we not just hire the best qualified for the job?**

In the 1990's many companies are trying to be serious about Affirmative Action again and whites are reacting negatively. It seems to me that companies often do not explain to their employees what they really mean by Affirmative

76

Action and so it is perceived to be just a quota system to be eligible for Federal projects. It is assumed that Affirmative Action lowers standards and hires people who are unqualified. When a woman or a person of color shows up in a new job, the other employees think she's only there because they need more women for their quota. They don't even consider she might have more qualifications than they do. Most often African-Americans have more education than the whites do on the same job.

Companies should make it very clear that they are not hiring or promoting people who are not qualified - they can't afford to hire people who are unproductive in this economy. The studies show that Affirmative Action has not lowered standards and that African-Americans are more likely to be employed in jobs below their capabilities.[31]

I think it's almost comical when white people are asking "Why don't we just hire the best qualified?" as though that was what we did before Affirmative Action. America has never hired people based on the best qualified. It always had more to do with your sex, your race and who recommended you. Even the assembly-line jobs and apprenticeship positions were given to friends and family members in the past. Whites learned about new openings from their friends and families before the job was even advertised. They were not hired because they could do the job; most were hired because they were seen as capable of being trained to do the job.

It's true that when Affirmative Action first started some companies took the easy way out and hired any Black who showed up, did not train them properly and then said Blacks can't do the job!

So, there have been cases where unqualified Blacks were hired or promoted; however, it seems logical to me to blame the person who did the hiring and took the easy way out instead of seriously recruiting from the Black community to get people who were qualified and making sure that they got the proper training and support to do the job. I've had many African-Americans share with me work situations where some of the whites they worked with did everything they could to make it difficult for them to do the job.

I know as a white woman, any new job situation is difficult and I've been in situations where the people I had to work with didn't want me there and tried to make me look incompetent. However, the fact that I was white meant that the people who hired me knew I was competent and supported my efforts. I would not have lasted without that support I got from the management level.

If we really did not have a racist/sexist system, then we could hire the best qualified; the way it is now whites (especially white males) have an advantage regardless of the qualifications; the people doing the hiring, even when they are trying to be fair, have been raised to see whites as superior (consciously or unconsciously) and thus bring these prejudices to the job. It's easy to convince yourself that the white man could do the job better.

I found it very interesting to see the anger expressed by whites (especially white males) when they began to allow a certain number of minorities and women into traditionally white and male colleges and medical schools. They complained that these people had lower grades than some of the white men who did not get in. It may be true that some of the African-Americans did have lower grades (though anyone applying for medical school has to have a certain level of achievement) but we forget that Blacks often were in schools where their teachers did not grade them fairly. I've had Black people tell me that they had white teachers who told them directly that they would not receive an A or that Blacks aren't as smart as whites. I know other Blacks who improved their confidence by writing papers for white students and getting A's on those and B's or C's on their own papers. They at least knew that they were just as capable as anyone. I know one Black woman whose grade point went up two points when the college started putting numbers on the papers instead of names so that the teachers did not know who wrote them.

The African-Americans and women do very well once they get into medical school and it is very important that we have minority and women doctors who have the empathy

78

necessary to serve the special needs that exist because of our system.

Colleges, and especially medical schools, have always had quotas and used them in the past as a way of keeping people out as well. Since Asians and Jewish people have traditionally had higher grades than most whites, quotas have been used to make sure only a small number of them were admitted. Colleges also have used quotas to make sure they got certain categories of students admitted; they have a certain number of alumni, a certain percentage of athletes, a certain number of foreign students, a certain number of students in their state and, certainly, a certain number of students who can actually pay without financial aid.

So here again, we only complain when quotas are applied to those we have not had to compete with in the past; it's hard for us to see that it's never been fair, never been based on just grades but more on your race, sex, origin and socio-economic status.

CONCLUSION

Many white Americans feel that Affirmative Action gives Blacks an unfair advantage and that there is no longer a need for it. They feel that it results in lowering standards and results in hiring unqualified people; research does not show this to be true.

We do not acknowledge the unfair advantages white people have because of their color, or that Blacks are still unemployed in record numbers proving that Affirmative Action has never been taken seriously.

We also don't really see how much discrimination has caused us to be less competitive in the world than the countries who use the talents of all their citizens.

White to White on Black/White

"To be defined by whites is to remain a slave."

Stokely Carmichael

Chapter 10

Identity

- **What do they want to be called? They keep changing it.**

African-Americans are in a unique position in America. They were brought here by the millions to be used as slaves. They were stripped of their original identity as much as possible in the inhumane and hideous process known as slave seasoning. They were separated from their own villagers and forbidden to speak any African languages. They were even forbidden to learn to read or write English; they had to learn to speak English from uneducated white overseers. They were not allowed to marry in most cases though often they performed their own marriage ceremonies. Blacks were systematically sold as property and families were continually broken up, most never to see each other again.

We can get maybe a glimpse of the pain and suffering and identity crisis these Africans must have gone through by what we know about the feelings of many adopted children. Until they are reconnected to their biological mother or father, they feel somewhat unfinished even though they love their adopted parents as mom and dad. They need to know where they came from to feel complete.

Not only were slaves separated from their immediate families but they also lost connection with their original land base, their language and traditions.

As most of us know from what has been written, Africans did not give up all of these things easily. Some even jumped ship on the way here rather than be slaves. They continued to fight back, run away and support each other's humanity.

We also know to a smaller degree what white people did to make Africans subservient and compliant. We know they were beaten but how many know that whites did very cruel and inhumane things in front of the others to make sure that they all knew what would happen if they did not obey. I'm talking about cutting off a hand or foot and cutting open a pregnant woman's stomach! It took a lot to make slaves out of Africans and yet they kept their humanity and dreams of being free some day.

Since whites thought of these Africans as property, they no longer referred to them as Africans; they began to call them "negroes", which really was a Portuguese/Spanish word for the color black. The subsequent inflections given to this word served to further degrade the people.

After slaves were emancipated, they were still called negroes and eventually they sought to get the word capitalized to Negro as we capitalized all others' ethnic origins. Once it was capitalized, they realized there were other problems with it.

The classification Negro had no history except for slavery; it had no land base to relate to and it was not a name that they chose for themselves. Anytime you allow someone else to define you, it serves their purpose to keep you in your place.

In the South, they had signs that used the words "colored" and "white" to let people know where they belonged but "colored" did not give Africans an identity; after all, everyone is colored, even whites!

So as Blacks began to find a new way (non-violent protest) to rebel against being treated as less than full human beings with rights of citizenship, they also came to the realization that being "Black" was the one thing that brought them together.

Identity

Also, during the Civil Rights Movement, they began to understand that "Black is beautiful" because it was Black people who were marching and fighting for America to live up to her stated values of "liberty and justice for all".

When we talk Black and white in America, we are not really talking colors; we are talking about groups of people with certain attitudes that bring them together in a racist society. Black values (often formed as a way to survive under oppression) are often in direct conflict with white American values. Black people are more co-operative while white people are more individualistic; Blacks are more people-oriented while whites are more property-oriented (America even developed bombs that would destroy people without hurting the buildings); Blacks are more concerned with a person's character while whites judge more quickly on color and social origins.

It is also my personal opinion, based on the many African-Americans that I've known, that they live up to the religious value of "loving one another as yourself" better than most white people who profess to believe it. In spite of all the injustices Blacks have endured, most are still trying to teach their children to love and not to hate even those who mistreat you. Obviously, not all Blacks manage to love whites in spite of the oppression but that should not be a surprise; the surprise is that most Blacks are still trying to love us and co-exist.

In the late 1980's, Black leadership decided that the next step to their identity process had to be to move towards being called African-American. You might wonder why they did not go directly to African-American from Negro but remember what the image was of Africa until recently by most of us. It was seen as the Dark Continent, uncivilized, with savages and cannibals ruled by Tarzan!

Now, we know that civilization began in Africa and that the Nile Valley was the high point of that. The Greek philosophers learned from Africans and eventually Europe developed a civilization based on what they learned from Africans. It's a heritage for Blacks to be proud of and a necessary part of the identity process.

White to White on Black/White

The immigrants who came here from Europe were called Italian-Americans, Irish-Americans, Polish-Americans, German-Americans, etc. for the first generations until they were finally accepted as Americans. Even now we have ethnic clubs that keep their heritage alive not to mention how we all celebrate St. Patrick's Day. Because the European immigrants came here knowing their heritage, they were able to bond together and use that solidarity to gain a voting block and therefore to share in the power of their communities.

That is what the call for Black Power was about during the Civil Rights Era; it was an attempt to unite and gain some control over what happened in their own communities so that Blacks could also share power with the whole.

African-Americans have found it difficult to have a good sense of their identity in America because they were continually treated as though they were less and left out of the history we teach in our schools. The history we teach in America has been very white, male, military and moneyed. Few others were given credit for their contributions. Even the Black History taught in schools has largely focused on inventions, rather than the human struggle of Blacks in America.

Eventually we will have to include all people in the history of America if we expect our children to grow up with a real appreciation of each other.

It's difficult for African-Americans to get a good sense of their own identity when they live in a country that makes them feel Black is bad; some children try to scrub the color from their skin and say when they grow up they want to be white and they prefer white dolls to play with over the Black dolls. Eventually they figure out that no matter how hard they try to be white that they're still not accepted and then may shift to being as aggressively Black as possible to retrieve their identity. In the end, many African-Americans begin to see the whole picture and identify with others in the world who are also oppressed.[32]

84

CONCLUSION

We need to have a better appreciation of how difficult it is for Blacks to have a good sense of their own identity in America when they live in a nation that continues to project Blacks as bad, aggressive and dangerous. How would you feel if people looked at you as a dangerous animal everytime they saw you?

Racism often causes the victims to have negative feelings of self-hatred, makes them blame themselves for not achieving, makes them feel like their lives are not valued and causes them to be so angry and frustrated that they can lose their respect for life.

The average person does not survive with a good sense of themselves in a racist system without serious family support and since racism also makes it more difficult to even have a family, many Blacks self-destruct. Whatever we don't like about African-Americans' attitudes or actions, our racist society has created!

African-Americans are still in the process of searching for an identity that gives them a history, a positive image, a land base and an international connection to economic possibilities.

It will take years to make the transition from Black to African-American complete. I think that when the name African-American is totally accepted it will yield a new sense of identity and power base for Blacks in America.

"Each year of delay in seriously and successfully attacking this problem makes it more difficult."

Workforce 2000

Chapter 11

SOLUTIONS

What can I do? The problem of racism is so complex and huge when you look at the whole system that it discourages many whites from doing anything. It seems that what little we can do won't matter. We wish we could just start all over tomorrow and do it right. However, it took a long time and lots of creative effort to create this mess and it will also take some long-term creative efforts to solve it!

We have to be committed for the long-term and do the small things that we can do. I found that in doing the small things I learned enough to do something a little larger. By doing the small things, we also are making others more aware and eventually we'll have enough people aware to elect some new leadership to help us do the rest.

I suggest that you start with the people you know who already care, the ones who will be the easiest to deal with. Small successes will help you to gain enough confidence to take on those people who are more difficult.

Also, don't expect everyone to be receptive. You can't change everyone; some people are totally closed to any new information on the issue. I also recommend that you don't make a family feud out of the issue. All of us have family members who are prejudiced. I recommend letting them know how you feel about it and that you'd appreciate it if they didn't speak that way because it's offensive to you. You can be a powerful role model by continuing to love them and at the same time exhibiting non-racist behavior and challenging as necessary.

You can continue to educate your extended family and set the example. Over a period of time, it will make a difference to those who are open. You can help them see that this generation of children will not succeed in the new, more diverse workforce if they don't fully accept and appreciate other people's differences.

It also is not productive to blame your parents for raising you racist, if that's the case. Most parents did the best they knew how and in their day it was more profitable to conform to the prejudice in order to lessen their children's problems; that is no longer true for our times. We will only limit our children's opportunities for the future.

The more your parents know about how you're rearing your children to be open to all races, the easier it also will be on them if your children end up in interracial relationships; it won't be such a surprise in that they will have had years to consider the possibility. Very few parents or grandparents are going to disown their children for their choices in the future.

The most important people to deal with on racism for many will be their spouses. It is difficult to rear your children to be non-racist if your spouse does not share your beliefs. When you have a spouse who is bigoted, you may be able to have an influence by sharing what you're reading, talking about the new more diverse workforce and expressing your concerns about the values you want your children to have. Appeal to the best values in your spouse; discuss what he/she was told when growing up or what experiences he/she had that caused him/her to have negative attitudes about a whole race. Chances are they've never had to face their insecurities that caused them to be prejudiced in their adult lives in any logical and rational manner.

If you're not getting anywhere with your spouse, perhaps there is a close friend who thinks more like you do who could have an influence if you recruited him/her to help.

If nothing works, you will have to do overtime to help your children understand that their other parent's attitude is not helpful for surviving in their generation, and help them understand the other parent's lack of appreciation for other races. Often men who are serious racists are also very sexist as well. If that is the case, women have to make a decision as to whether or not they want to be owned their whole lives and what effect that relationship will have on their children's future.

There are many ways that white people can influence others. Everyone will not feel comfortable doing the same things but everyone can contribute something.

I highly recommend balancing what you do so that your main focus is on changing white people while you also do some things that will provide you opportunities for interaction with African-Americans.

On a personal level, you could subscribe or read Black magazines to help you be more aware, you can buy books and dolls that represent other races for your children or grandchildren. You might enroll your children in programs or camps that will give them interaction with other races. You might volunteer to help with an orphanage or be a big brother or big sister to an African-American child.

Usually pre-school children learn a lot about people of color by your reactions to their questions. Invariably little children ask those questions in public places! The typical reaction of a parent is to be so embarrassed that he/she puts his/her hand over the child's mouth and gets away quickly. That tells the children that there is something bad or scary about people of color and that they shouldn't ask any more questions.

I find it much more productive to deal matter-of-factly right there with the question. When you say, "Yes, that's a Black person; people come in all colors and sizes"; then you leave the child open to other questions and don't frighten them and, of course, the Black person they're referring to will feel better that you dealt with it out front.

One of my favorite stories on children that someone shared with me was about a kindergarten student (a little white girl with no association with other races). Her school was going to have a kindergarten class from a Black school join them for the afternoon. Her parents had talked negatively about the idea and yet dressed her up special for the occasion. She was standing in the corner of the school playground looking very fearful when a little Black girl approached her and asked why she looked so scared. The little white girl said she was afraid because "the Blacks" were coming. The poor thing had no idea who "the Blacks" were - her parents had her expecting monsters; she had no idea this little Black girl she was sharing her feelings with was someone to fear!

It's natural for children to notice differences and ask questions; however, they don't see difference as negative unless they're told by adults that it is. It's also important to explain to children early that even though color shouldn't make a difference that some people treat people badly because of their color, and this is wrong. Be honest!

You should share your new learnings with your family, friends, co-workers and try to get them involved as well.

You could visit a Black or interracial church. You can volunteer to tutor or coach Black children or help with poverty programs.

You also need to investigate what kind of history your children are being taught and try to get the schools to tell the history of all contributors to America and to explain what racism is and how it destroys people of color in America. Little children are very willing to do the right thing - they take littering seriously when they're taught about it - they will hide their parents cigarettes when they're told smoking is bad! So why not explain about racism so that they can grow up being part of the solution?

Recommend in-service training for your teachers on racism and challenge them if they have the children doing plays or projects that put down or perpetuate stereotypes. Often the teachers do not realize how things are prejudiced and try to correct their errors when approached constructively. Any serious displays of racism can be dealt with by writing the person a letter with a copy to the principal and superintendent registering your dismay and shock that your children's teachers are setting such a bad example.

I once had remarkable results from this approach. The superintendent called the principal and said "What is this? We don't want any bad publicity, take care of it." The principal called the teacher and said the same thing to him and the teacher immediately called me and wanted to talk.

We got together and, much to his credit, he confirmed by talking to a Black man he knew that what I was saying was true. He had no idea that he was being offensive! He apologized and got the Drama Club to agree that they would be careful to not promote stereotypes in the future. One person can make a difference - the small things add up and make others more aware!

If you're in a major city where equal education is not given to all sections of your city, check out some of the new alternative schools that have worked so well in several places (Read Reinventing Government - see Recommended Reading List). All of our children should get a good education regardless of their income level so that they can be productive adults. Support your public schools because they have the best potential for the real purpose of education in America - to help prepare our children for their future roles of becoming informed citizens in a democracy with an appreciation of all the people who make up America.

We know how to bring students together; they can be assigned projects where each has a part to contribute to the whole or we can have each group fully represented on social and student government committees. The interaction needs to be there for students to really get to know each other and find they can work together for the good of the whole.

Make sure that your school and public libraries have a good selection of books and magazines on other races so that children have more exposure.

There are also a number of things you can do in your work situation to make a difference. Pay more attention to how minorities and women are treated and give them support when necessary. Try to have more interaction with minorities and include the people you like in your social life, the same as you do with whites. Make sure that people know what your views are on racism and sexism when the subject comes up. Let co-workers know that racial and/or sexual remarks are offensive and inappropriate.

Of course, if you're the "boss", you also can make sure that your employees know that racism and sexism will not be tolerated at work. You also should make clear your stand on Affirmative Action so that they know any new employee or one who gets a promotion will be qualified for the job and should be supported.

Often, on the job, you may have an African-American that you clash with - it's sometimes difficult to know if it is a racial issue or just different personalities that cause the clash. Before you write off the person, try bringing it out in the open. Ask if you've done something to offend; say you'd like to know so that you can correct it as you have been working on your prejudice and would like to have a better working relationship and get to know him/her better. Even if your personality differences make it impossible to be friends, it will earn some respect for you by trying to be honest. Most of our interpersonal conflicts come from not bringing the problems out in the open - they tend to get worse, not better!

A white male executive once shared this story with me. He said that he came into his office one day and two of his employees (a white woman and a Black woman) were having a knock-down, drag-out fight. He broke them up and asked what was going on here? One of the women said that the other woman took her pencil!! He concluded that "women will fight over anything"!

As it turned out, he did not realize what had transpired between these women over the past year. It was very much a racial issue; they had been going back and forth at each other verbally for a long time. The pencil was the "straw that broke the camel's back" - people don't fight over a pencil! It's always wise to find out what is behind any issue when someone blows up over something that's not really important, especially if race is involved.

If you work for a large company, volunteer to serve on an

employees' committee that deals with the issues of racial and sexual issues; you will learn a lot and make some friends. It's always important to have a support system when you deal with the issues of racism or sexism. Otherwise, you may think that you're the only one who cares and give up too easily.

Of course, the other thing we all can do is to find out where our government and school officials stand on racism and sexism and how they vote on the issues that are connected. Let them know your views - often our Congress members send surveys to us for our comments - tell them your concerns. Needless to say, vote accordingly, and do vote even if it is only for the lesser of two evils!

If you're politically active, consider running yourself - you can reach more people and cause them to be more aware of how our future is threatened by continuing a system that does not have full participation of all its citizens.

Remember also whether you're dealing with your family, church, school, work or government, numbers matter! I guarantee you if you show up at a school board meeting with 300 people or at your boss's office with twenty employees (or less, depending on the size of your workforce), they will listen in a whole different way to your complaints. They have to say that the community (or workforce) is upset, not just some person who likes to complain.

We do have power in America, we've just given it up because we don't organize it. I learned when I first got involved with racism that often the "bad guys" win because they're better organized, more verbal and have a strategy. It's time for us to do the same! Let's take back America for all of its people, not just a few.

Also, don't forget your sense of humor! I'm not talking about jokes; I'm talking about being able to laugh at yourself when you try and don't succeed. If you keep your sense of humor, you can get up and try again! Sometimes you can even hear a racist remark and respond to it as though it was positive. For instance, if you hear someone say about Blacks, "They're everywhere, can't go anywhere without running into one!" You can say, "Yes, isn't it great, isn't it about time?"

You can then walk away and at least leave them confused; they won't be comfortable saying it to anyone else and will have to start thinking maybe things have changed. Don't lose them, at least confuse them. We don't always have a lot of time to spend on a person so even the little things count.

Now when you want or need to really convince someone and you're willing to spend some time on it, there is a method that helps you to approach the issue logically and takes the argument out of it. This method also works on other issues and spouses as well! I don't know who to give credit for the original outline but we (Dr. Charles H. King, Jr. and Associates) developed it at the Urban Crisis Center in the early 1970's to help challenge people on racism.

Ten Step Challenge

1. **State Your Opinion; Be Concise**.

   You make people defensive if you start out with questions so first tell them your opinion (it's always helpful to let people know "Where You're Coming From"). Keep it short so they can't pick out something to change the subject with.

2. **Get General Agreement**.

   Most people will agree in general how things should be. Most will agree it would be nice if we did get along and it would be better if we didn't have racism.

   When you can get agreement in general, then your only disagreements will be over how do we get there. It gives you a positive goal to work towards.

Solutions

3. **State the Crisis.**

Since people often do not have a lot of information on the issue, they often don't know how bad things really are. You need to give them some solid statistics and facts. There are some sources in the bibliography and the newspapers and news magazines publish any latest information. Begin to look for articles that will help you explain the crisis.

4. **Project the Crisis.**

As Americans, we're not very good at dealing with things in the too distant future. So help people see that this crisis is already here and how we deal with it in this decade will determine America's future and that of our children.

5. **Do Not Argue.**

At this point, you may begin to get some disagreement. Be careful not to allow it to turn into an argument! It's easy to end up arguing but it's not really constructive - your ego gets all involved and you may not even talk to each other again.

6. **Leave Them Thinking.**

People need some reflection time when given much new information, so leave them with something to read, if possible, that helps explain your view. Ask them "Would you mind reading this? I'd like to see what you think after you've had a chance to think about it."

7. **Schedule Another Time to Get Together**.

If you set up another time to get together, people will more likely be serious and read your article and formulate some opinions. Often you can be very casual about getting back together if it's someone you see on a regular basis. You could make time at lunch, after work or after a meeting.

8. **<u>Know the Person's Value System</u>**.

Fortunately in America, most people have value systems that are good - if we all lived up to them, we wouldn't have such a serious problem. So, if you know you're dealing with a person who has a religious value system, you can use Bible verses and cause them to question if they live up to what they say they believe. Do they really believe "We're all created equal" or that we should "love one another" or that we should "love our neighbors"?

Almost all religions have love as a base and would not approve of treating anyone as less than human.

Of course, not everyone has a religious base. Sometimes, you may be talking to someone who is very patriotic and it might be more effective to discuss how racism affects the image of America. How much longer can we tell other countries what to do about human rights when we can't even give our own citizens human rights?

Remember, our institutions also have a value system; largely economic values. So begin to figure out how you will make money or lose money depending on how your institution deals with racism and sexism. Companies have found that people are more

productive when the company makes it clear that all will
be appreciated and valued.

Remember, too, what I said earlier about organizing.
If you find a policy that you think is discriminatory
in your work place, ask around and see if others will
agree with you. Then the boss has to say the
workforce has a problem with the policy, not just an
individual.

9. **Reverse and Personalize the Situation**.

Ask the person what they would do if someone
mistreated them or someone they loved regularly? If
you can get them to start thinking on a personal
level, the solutions will be more obvious and serious.
We know for sure if someone told us our children
would not get an equal education or chance at life,
we'd have a fit and be active about solving the
problem.

Sometimes this will work all by itself if you're
dealing with someone who is already somewhat
understanding.

10. **Never Argue with a Bigot**.

If you've gone through all of the above and the
person is still repeating the same thing and doesn't
show any signs of considering anything you've said,
then chances are you have a person who has a closed
mind on the issue. You won't be able to get to
everyone; just go on to someone else or find
someone you think he/she might listen to.

Also, start with a person who will be easier to get through
to until you get better and more confident about your

responses. Practice eventually causes you to have automatic responses as you begin to see the patterns involved in the questions.

CONCLUSION

If you don't want to be part of the problem of racism, you can be part of the solution.

There are many things that we all can do towards changing our people and institutions that will have a snowball effect on our communities, country and our children's future. Celebrate both your victories and defeats because you never really lose if you cause people to confront themselves on the issue.

Start small and work your way up to the larger things as you grow. It's clear to me from my own experience in ridding myself, my husband, and my children from racism and sexism, that you do "reap what you sow". You can have a much better marriage, raise much better children and look yourself in the mirror in the morning knowing that you're trying your best to be part of the solution.

Maybe as an individual I can't change the world but I certainly have changed many of the people I came in contact with and my community and so can you!

Chapter 12

OUR FUTURE

As Edmond Burke said "the only thing necessary for the triumph of evil is for good men to do nothing."[33]

That pretty much sums up racism in America. We are losing our freedom and democracy because we are not living up to what we say we believe about equality and justice. As whites, we are very much a part of the problem if we're not trying to change ourselves and those around us.

While we think we are free in America, the truth is we have given up much of our independence by conforming to a racist system that does it for us. If we go along with the peer pressure that keeps us silent when others are putting Blacks or others down by negative remarks and jokes, then we also become less. If we are really free then we should be able to stand up for our beliefs and relate to and love all people.

We also lose our freedom by helping our children to go along with a racist system instead of making them strong enough to think for themselves and have enough self-esteem that they don't have to get their identity by thinking that they are superior.

As Americans, we need to begin to see the possibilities of what America could be and ought to be. To really admit that we are a racist country is to begin to change it. It may have been economically feasible to have slaves in the past but it is certainly not to anyone's advantage to keep the old master/slave relationship going now.

As Dr. Martin Luther King, Jr. said in I Have a Dream,[34] our destiny and freedom as Blacks and whites in America are very much tied together. Anytime you set one group up as superior, you don't even consider the talents of others. We are losing in America because we allow racism to keep us from using the talents of all our citizens.

At a time when business is trying to have a team-directed workforce, and to humanize the workforce in order to be more productive, we must begin to question our old ways of thinking about what is strong and what is weak. Is it really strong to just do what you're told, and weak if you care or question? We've tried being very liberal and we've tried being very conservative; it's time to have a very different way of thinking if we are to survive as a real leader for democracy in the world.

It's not enough just to take care of people or give them things; it also does not make sense to deny that our system is designed to keep certain groups out of the mainstream and dependent. It's time to design our programs to help people be self-sufficient, not dependent. Then they can better add to our economy and make us more competitive.

I think that the same things that happen to individuals who try hard to eliminate racism and sexism from their lives and thoughts can also happen to America. It's a very character-building, freeing experience and allows one to have more appreciation and empathy for all human beings; when people feel valued, they naturally want to contribute their talents for the good of all.

America is made up of a very diverse population (people from all over the world are our citizens); that should be an asset! However, racism and sexism have kept us from appreciating our differences and so it has also kept us from using the talents of all our citizens. We no longer can afford to promote divisions; if we are to continue as a free country and a real leader in the world, we have to all become Americans working together to solve the many problems facing us today.

Racism is the major social problem in the United States

today and we have an individual and collective responsibility to address it in order to avoid disaster and secure our future.

How we commit to change in this decade will decide our future; if we do not find ways to use our citizens more fully and make our government operate more realistically, we will all suffer. Our worst enemy is our limited view of what is possible if we really have full participation of all of our citizens.

"Racism which diminishes its object to non-human status, also diminishes its perpetrators, all are losers by its terms."

White Racism: A Psycho-History

ENDNOTES

1. Benjamin P. Bowser and Raymond G. Hunt, eds., Impacts of Racism on White America, Sage Publications, 1981, page 116

2. Joel Kovel, White Racism: A Psycho History, Pantheon Books, 1970, page 34

3. Jawanza Kunjufu, Countering the Conspiracy to Destroy Black Boys, African-American Images, 1985, page viii

4. Erich Fromm, Anatomy of Human Destructiveness, Holt, Rinehart and Winston, New York, 1973, page 108

5. Jawanza Kunjufu, Countering the Conspiracy to Destroy Black Boys, African-American Images, 1985, page 24

6. Gerald Jaynes and Robin Williams, eds., A Common Destiny: Blacks and American Society, National Academy Press, 1989, page 23

7. John F. Dovidio and Samuel Gaentner, eds., Prejudice, Discrimination and Racism, Academic Press, 1986, page 260

8 . George Eaton Simpson and Milton J. Yinger, Racial and Cultural Minorities - An Analysis of Prejudice and Discrimination, Chatham Publishers, 1985, page 275

9 . Louis L. Knowles and Kenneth Prewitt, Institutional Racism, Prentice-Hall, 1969, page 58

10 . Gerald Jaynes and Robin Williams, eds., A Common Destiny: Blacks and America Society, National Academy Press, 1989, page 8

11 . Andrew Hacker, Two Nations, Charles Scribner's Sons, 1992, page 75

12 . Roy L. Brooks, Rethinking the American Race Problem, University of California Press, 1990, page 81

13 . Gerald Jaynes and Robin Williams, eds., A Common Destiny: Blacks and American Society, National Academy Press, 1989, page 11

14 . Ibid, page 21

15 . Gerald Jaynes and Robin Williams, eds., A Common Destiny: Blacks and American Society, National Academy Press, 1989, page 15

16 . Benjamin P. Bowser and Raymond G. Hunt, eds., Impacts of Racism on White America, Sage Publications, 1981, page 115

White to White on Black/White

Publications, 1981, page 115

17. Terrence Deal and Allan A. Kennedy, <u>Corporate Cultures</u>, Addison-Wesley, 1982, page 78

18. Joel Kovel, <u>White Racism: A Psycho History</u>, Pantheon Books, 1970, page 86

19. Bob Blauner, <u>Black Lives, White Lives</u>, University of California Press, 1989, page 315

20. James M. Jones, <u>Prejudice and Racism</u>, Addison-Wesley Publishing, 1972, page 118

21. Andrew Hacker, <u>Two Nations</u>, Charles Scribner's Sons, 1992, page 96

22. Gerald Jaynes and Robin Williams, eds., <u>A Common Destiny: Blacks and American Society</u>, National Academy Press, 1989, page 532

23. Andrew Hacker, <u>Two Nations</u>. Charles Scribner's Sons, 1992, page 88

24. Ibid, page 81

25. David Osborne and Ted Gaebler, <u>Reinventing Government</u>, Addison-Wesley Publishing, 1992, page 28

26. Gerald Jaynes and Robin Williams, eds., <u>A Common Destiny: Blacks and American Society</u>, National Academy Press, 1989, page 8

27. Laford Porter and Bernard Mohr, eds., <u>Reading Book for Human Relations Training</u>, NTL,

Endnotes

Arlington, Virginia, 1988, page 28

28. Gunner Myrdal, American Dilemma: The Negro Problem and Modern Democracy, Harper and Brothers, 1944

29. Workforce 2000, Department of Labor, Hudson Institute, 1987, xiii

30. Money Magazine, "Money and Race", December, 1989

31. Benjamin P. Bowser and Raymond G. Hunt, eds., Impacts of Racism on White America, Sage Publications, 1981, page 43

32. Joseph L. White, The Psychology of Blacks: An Afro-American Perspective, Prentice-Hall, 1984, page 9, 10

33. Rollo May, Carl Rogers, Maslow, Abraham, etal. Politics and Innocence: A Humanistic Debate, Saybrook Publishers, Texas, 1986, page 13

34. Clint Bolick, Changing Course, Transaction Books, 1988, pages 46, 47

RECOMMENDED READING

THEORY/ANALYZATIONS:

Impacts of Racism on White America. Bowser, Benjamin P. and Hunt, Raymond G., Editors. Sage Publications. Beverly Hills, California, 1981.

Majority and Minority: The Dynamics of Racial and Ethnic Relations. Yetman, Norman R. and Steele, C. Hoy, Editors. Allyn and Bacon, Inc. Boston, Massachusetts, 1971.

Wellman, David T. Portraits of White Racism. Cambridge University Press, New York, 1977.

Yeboah, Samuel Kennedy. The Ideology of Racism. Hansib Publishers, Ltd. London, 1988.

HISTORY OF ATTITUDES

Caditz, Judith. White Liberals in Transition. Spectrum Publishers, Inc. New York, 1976.

Jones, James M. Prejudice and Racism. Addison-Wesley Publishing Co. Menlo Park, California, 1972.

Pinkney, Alphonso. The Myth of Black Progress. Cambridge University Press. New York, 1984.

Schuman, Howard, Steel, Charlotte and Bobo, Lawrence. Racial Attitudes in America. Harvard University Press. Boston, Massachusetts, 1985.

BLACK HISTORY

Bennett, Lerone. Before the Mayflower. Johnson Publishing. Chicago, 1969.

Recommended Reading

Bradley, Michael. The Black Discovery of America. Toronto: Personal Library, 1981.

Haley, Alex. Roots. Dell Publishing. New York, 1977.

Harding, Vincent. There is a River. Vintage Books. New York, 1983.

Van Sertima, Ivan. They Came Before Columbus: The African Presence in America. Random House. New York, 1977.

Video. Eyes on the Prize. PBS, 1986.

INTERRACIAL MARRIAGE/SEX

Stember, Charles H. Sexual Racism: The Emotional Barrier to an Integrated Society. Elsevier. New York, 1976.

Washington, Joseph R. Marriage in Black and White. Beacon Press. Boston, 1970.

STATISTICS

A Common Destiny: Blacks and American Society. Jaynes, Gerald David and Williams, Jr., Robin M., Editors. National Academy Press. Washington, D.C., 1989.

*Hacker, Andrew. Two Nations. Charles Scribner's Sons. New York, 1992.

*Kozol, Jonathan. Savage Inequalities. Crown Publishers, Inc. New York, 1991.

Rothenberg, Paula S. Racism and Sexism, An Integrated Study. St. Martin's Press. New York, 1988.

*Workforce 2000. Johnston, William B., Project Director. Department of Labor. Hudson Institute, Inc. Indianapolis, Indiana, June, 1987.

SOLUTIONS

Intergroup and Minority Relations: An Experiential Handbook. Fromkin, Howard L. and Sherwood, John J. Editors. University Associates, Inc. LaJolla, California, 1976.

Katz, Judy H. White Awareness: Handbook for Anti-racism Training. University of Oklahoma Press. Norman, Oklahoma, 1978.

Kunjufu, Jawanza. Countering the Conspiracy to Destroy Black Boys. African American Images. Chicago, 1985.

*Osborne, David and Gaebler, Ted. Reinventing Government Addison-Wesley Publishing Company. Reading, Massachusetts, 1992.

MALE/FEMALE

Byers, Kenneth. Man in Transition. Journeys Together. LaMesa, California, 1990.

Schaef, Anne Wilson. Womens Reality. Harper and Row Publishers. San Francisco, California, 1985.

Tannen, Deborah. You Just Don't Understand. Morrow. New York, 1990.

MISCELLANEOUS

Davis, George and Watson, Glegg. Black Life in Corporate America. Anchor Press. New York, 1979.

Recommended Reading

Kotlowitz, Alex. There Are No Children Here. Doubleday. New York, 1991.

* Ryan, William. Blaming the Victim. Pantheon. New York, 1971.

Terkel, Studs. Race. The New Press. New York, 1992.

* Must Reading

MATERIAL FROM ORGANIZATIONS

Southern Poverty Law Center
400 Washington Avenue
Montgomery, AL 36104

- Klanwatch Project
- "Teaching Tolerance" Magazine
 (Free to Teachers)

Center for Democratic Renewal
P.O. Box 50469
Atlanta, GA 30302

- "When Hate Groups Come To Town" (Handbook)

Children's Defense Fund
25 "E" Street, N.W.
Washington, D.C. 20001

- "State of America's Children" Report

Clergy and Laity Concerned
340 Mead Road
Atlanta, GA 30030

- "CALC Report"

BIBLIOGRAPHY

A Common Destiny: Blacks and American Society. Jaynes, Gerald David and Williams, Jr., Robin M., Editors. National Academy Press. Washington, D.C. 1989.

Blauner, Bob. Black Lives, White Lives. University of California Press. Berkeley, California, 1989.

Bolick, Clint. Changing Course. Transaction Books. New Brunswick, U.S.A., 1988.

Brooks, Roy L. Rethinking The American Race Problem. University of California Press. Los Angeles, California, 1990.

Deal, Terrence and Kennedy, Allan A. Corporate Cultures. Addison-Wesley Publishing Co. Massachusetts, 1982.

Fromm, Erich. Anatomy of Human Destructiveness. Holt, Rinehart and Winston. New York, 1973.

Hacker, Andrew. Two Nations. Charles Scribner's Sons. New York, 1992.

Impacts of Racism on White America. Bowser, Benjamin P. and Hunt, Raymond G., Editors. Sage Publications. Beverly Hills, California, 1981.

Jones, James M. Prejudice and Racism. Addison-Wesley Publishing Co. Menlo Park, California, 1972.

Knowles, Louis L. and Prewitt, Kenneth. Institutional Racism in America. Prentice-Hall, Inc. New Jersey, 1969.

Kovel, Joel. White Racism: A Psycho History. Pantheon Books. New York, 1970.

Bibliography

Kunjufu, Jawanza. Countering the Conspiracy to Destroy Black Boys. African American Images. Chicago, 1985.

May, Rollo, Rogers, Carl, Maslow, Abraham, et al. Politics and Innocence: A Humanistic Debate. Saybrook Publishers. Texas, 1986.

Money Magazine. "Money and Race". December, 1989.

Myrdal, Gunner. American Dilemma: The Negro Problem and Modern Democracy. Harper and Brothers. New York, 1944.

Osborne, David and Gaebler, Ted. Reinventing Government. Addison-Wesley Publishing Company. Reading, Massachusetts, 1992.

Prejudice, Discrimination and Racism. Dovidio, John F. and Gaertner, Samuel, Editors. Academic Press, Inc. New York, 1986.

Reading Book for Human Relations Training. Porter, Lawrence and Mohr, Bernard, editors. National Training Labs. Arlington, Virginia, 1988.

Simpson, George Eaton and Yinger, J. Milton. Racial and Cultural Minorities - An Analysis of Prejudice and Discrimination. Plenum Press. New York, 1985.

White, Joseph L. The Psychology of Blacks: An Afro-American Perspective. Prentice-Hall, Inc. New Jersey, 1984.

Workforce 2000. Johnston, William B., Project Director. Department of Labor. Hudson Institute, Inc. Indianapolis, Indiana, June, 1987.

Also available by Toni E. Weaver, Ph.D.

Listing of Multi-Cultural Books for Children

A 28 page booklet to help you choose books that will give your children an appreciation of other cultures or help them learn more about their own. Includes listings for African-Americans, Hispanic-Americans, Asian-Americans and Native-Americans for ages Preschool through Sixth Grade. This booklet also includes some resources for educators and parents.

ORDER FORM

VOICES PUBLISHING hopes you have found this book a valuable resource. For ordering additional copies or further information on racism workshops and speaking availability of Dr. Weaver, please return this form to:

VOICES PUBLISHING
P.O. Box 13-V
Vandalia, OH 45377-0013

- -

Please send me the following:

____Copies of **White to White on Black/white**
@$9.95 each $_____

____Copies of **"Listing of Multi-Cultural Books for Children"** @$2.25 each $_____

Shipping/Handling: $2.00 for the first book and $.75 for each additional book.
$.60 each for each "Listing of Multi-Cultural Books for Children." $_____

Ohioans: Please add 6.5% Sales Tax $_____
                (on printed material only)
TOTAL ENCLOSED $_____

____Information on racism workshops

____Speaking availability of Dr. Toni E. Weaver

Ship to: (Please Print)

Name: _____

Address: _____

_____

Allow 3-4 weeks for delivery